HANS BLOMQUIST

IN THE MOOD
FOR COLOUR

perfect palettes for creative interiors

photography by
DEBI TRELOAR & HANS BLOMQUIST

RYLAND PETERS & SMALL
LONDON • NEW YORK

Designer Megan Smith
Senior Commissioning Editor
Annabel Morgan
Editor Zia Mattocks
Production Controller
Gordana Simakovic

Art Director Leslie Harrington
Editorial Director Julia Charles
Publisher Cindy Richards

Indexer Hilary Bird

First published in 2016 by
Ryland Peters & Small
20–21 Jockey's Fields,
London WC1R 4BW
and
Ryland Peters & Small, Inc.
341 E 116th St,
New York, NY 10029
www.rylandpeters.com

10 9 8 7 6 5 4 3 2 1

Text © Hans Blomquist 2016
Design and photography
© Ryland Peters & Small 2016

ISBN 978 1 84975 755 3

A catalogue record for this book is available
from the British Library.

US Library of Congress cataloging-in-
publication data has been applied for.

Printed and bound in China

CONTENTS

INTRODUCTION   6

A WORLD FULL OF COLOUR   10

DARK   14

PALE   58

NATURAL   98

SOFT   128

BOLD   172

Address book   202

Credits   203

Index   206

Merci   208

INTRODUCTION

When it comes to colour and how to work with it, there are quite a few self-designated 'experts' around who are full of rules and regulations about which shades to choose, how to work with them, which ones can be combined and so on. Trust me when I say that there's no right or wrong when it comes to choosing colours. Only you are qualified to decide what suits you best.

It might sound easy for me to say this as I am an interiors stylist and, during the course of my job, have learnt how best to decorate rooms to create a particular effect. Well, thanks to my experience, I can tell you that creating a scheme you love is not as hard as you might think. But you do have to be brave enough to trust your instincts, go for what you like and put it together in your own way. As with so much in life, confidence is the key – the confidence to choose colours you love. Many of us are timid when it comes to colour choices, but if you compromise you may regret it. Sometimes it's hard to be brave but the good news is that it's only paint – if you hate it, you can paint over it again!

There are a few things to bear in mind. Consider the natural light in your home. Northern light is cool and blue so can make a space look cold and stark. Darker, richer shades work well in this sort of light. Southern light is golden and bright and makes almost any colour look good, but be warned that whites can look creamy and greys turn to beige. I always use a tester pot on a piece of lining paper to get a good idea of the end result.

I have tried to make this book as personal and inspirational as possible. There are literally hundreds of different ideas for colour schemes as well as suggestions for imaginative ways to add colour to your home. I do so hope you will enjoy reading it and find it useful. Let's bring more colour into the world and make it a happier, more colourful place to live in!

In my work as an art director and interiors stylist, I'm always looking out for new colours and paint brands. I have a few favourites that offer an excellent selection of colours: Farrow & Ball, Little Greene and Benjamin Moore. What I like about these paints is that they have a very matt finish, which gives a soft, velvety look.

Another paint company that I love is Bauwerk Colour, an Australian company producing eco-friendly modern lime paint. We photographed the wonderful German castle of the owners, Bronwyn and Andreas Riedel, for this book. A little later, I was thrilled to receive an email from them asking if I would be interested in creating my own range of paint colours for Bauwerk – probably one of the most exciting and flattering requests I have ever received!

Some colours in my new range are influenced by places I have visited – for example, Tucson is a tribute to a sage green shade seen on a trip to Arizona. But, as always, I draw most of my inspiration from nature and have created shades such as Tumble, Misty and Dusty. Drift was inspired by our whippet, Felix, who has the most beautiful velvety mushroom-coloured coat. The colours are fairly neutral so will work well in any interior and, thanks to the lime paint formulation, they all have a chalky feel that looks wonderful when used on a large scale.

Mixing colours can be done in a million different ways but with Bronwyn at Bauwerk Colour I am in safe hands, as her knowledge of mixing paint is extraordinary. I am thrilled to be part of such an exciting collaboration.

NINE COLOURS.

The first samples of my new paint range were finished just in time for us to feature them in this book, although the finished colours may vary slightly from the ones shown here. On this page, a canvas has been loosely painted with a coat of Tumble. Opposite, Tumble hangs on the wall, the large blue canvas is Dyed and the brown canvas at the front is Mudd.

A WORLD FULL OF COLOUR

It's easy to take colour for granted. We forget to appreciate the amazing, dazzling world that surrounds us, full of a million different shades that have the power to lift our spirits or soothe our moods. For my job, I'm lucky enough to travel the world and colour surprises me wherever I go – I'm often transfixed by the different colours and light I've experienced in different parts of the globe. And, as I have mentioned before, most of my inspiration comes from the colours of the natural world.

So the next time you leave your house, whether you are passing through familiar landscapes or visiting a different country, look around and marvel at the variety of the colours that surround you. Now every smartphone has a camera, it's easy to pull it out on the spur of the moment and record whatever catches your eye. Over the past couple of years, I've amassed a huge collection of pictures that display a wide range of different colours and textures and these are a rich source of inspiration. Try it yourself – next time you're seeking colour inspiration, flick through your phone pics and note which ones that you instinctly like best.

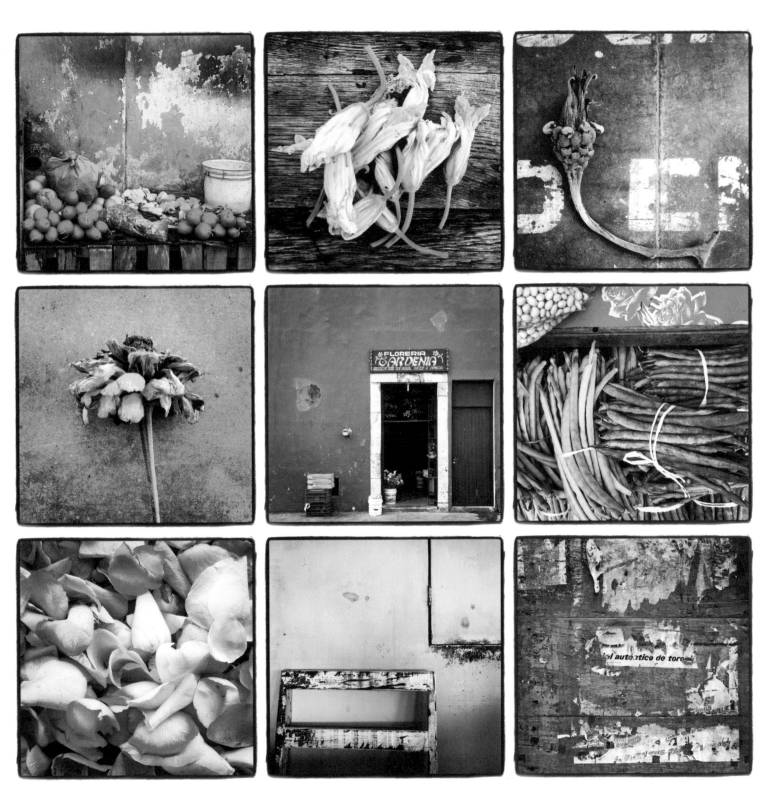

I spend a lot of time taking pictures with my phone when I am travelling and there is beauty to be found nearly everywhere you go. A trip to Mexico sparked a new love for vibrant, saturated hues like yellow and red. Nature always inspires me with its wonderful colour combinations, such as the green and red pea pods (centre right) and the yellow and green of the courgette/zucchini flowers (top centre).

Nature is my starting point for any interior project. There is a never-ending source of colour inspiration on offer wherever you look – these dried leaves, pumpkins, ears of corn and seashells are just a few of my favourite shades. The pictures here were taken in different parts of the world, such as Tulum in Mexico, Barcelona, Cape Town, Stockholm and the south of France.

Any worn or distressed texture is guaranteed to catch my eye immediately, especially if there's some colour still clinging to the surface. I saw the door at the top left in a restaurant in Mexico. Whenever I travel I visit the local food market, as I am intrigued by vegetables and fruits I have never seen before. Dried palm leaves and a vintage rope provide useful inspiration for both colour and texture.

Dark and moody colours can be hard to digest for some but are loved by others, while many people may long to try them but don't dare to take the bold step of adding deeper shades to their home. I am a huge fan of dark colours and wish I had used more of them in my own home. They have such impact and create a sense of drama yet at the same time give a very calm and cocooning feeling. The different dark pigments to choose from include deepest indigo, inky black, thunder grey and earthy brown shades. Variations on these colours will work well with any style of architecture and décor, whether your home is super-modern or more traditional.

DARK

DARK INSPIRATIONS

Nature is a rich source of inspiration for dark colours, even if that doesn't seem to be the case on a bright summer's day, when green leaves and colourful flowers are in abundance. But towards the end of summer, these vivid hues begin to fade and moodier colours start to appear. As a summer-loving person, I don't really like the transition from summer to autumn, when the long, hot days give way to dark, cool evenings, but I do prefer the richer colour palette that autumn brings. Maybe this is because an autumnal colour scheme is so much more muted and relaxing to look at, as it all sits together so harmoniously – the burnt-orange leaves on the dark brown earth, with the chestnuts piling up as the trees lose their fruit. This is when I find most of my inspiration for new ways of using colour, as these dark tones make such great and versatile backdrops.

As a summer-loving person, I don't really like the transition from summer to autumn, when the long, hot days give way to dark, cool evenings, but I do prefer the richer colour palette that autumn brings.

DESIGNED BY NATURE.

It amazes me that all the colours around us are designed by nature. If you have read my previous books, you will already know how much I love nature, and now, after working on this book, I find that I love it even more. I might be stating the obvious when I say that the colours we surround ourselves with are inspired by what we find in nature, but I do think most of us forget to thank her for it. Shown here are just a few of nature's many treasures: stems of beautiful, bright blue berries from a *Viburnum dentatum* 'Blue muffin' bush; bundles of branches from a birch tree, which make the perfect kindling for a log fire; a dish of velvety blueberries; and a pile of smooth, glossy chestnuts. All of these colours work well in any interior.

MOODY BLUES

I have always been a denim fan – I love jeans, not only for their durability but also for their wonderful colour. I always buy unwashed jeans, as their rich, nearly black indigo hue is so beautiful. Anything goes with deep, moody blues – light or dark, muted tones or bright, clear, spring-like shades. In an interior, dark blue works as a neutral and looks brilliant either covering the walls or when used as a grounding accent in the form of textiles and decorative objects. I especially like to layer different shades of blue, from darkest navy to washed-out cornflower. There is nothing more comfortable to wear than denim, and it is just as comfortable to live in a moody blue interior.

BLUE INSPIRATION.
To help you decide what blue to go for, collect samples in different shades, or paint paper or canvas using tester pots and hang it up. Here, I used Midnight and Abysse by Flamant, Deep Space Blue by Little Greene and Drawing Room Blue by Farrow & Ball.

USED DENIM.
I can never throw away jeans, even when they are past their best, and I used some old pairs to make this patchwork cloth (overleaf). The wall is Railings by Farrow & Ball.

MONOCHROME.

The different textures and shades of moody blues play against each other very successfully, creating a look that is interesting, inviting and very calming (previous spread).

TESTING COLOURS.

At one stage while I was working on this book, our apartment was full of painted canvases, either taped to the wall or hanging on lengths of string (opposite). This was the easiest way for me to test the various colours that I wanted to use. The painting of the peony on the far right is by my dear friend Kristin Perers.

MIX WITH NATURE.

This birch sofa was bought as a prop for a photoshoot and I didn't plan to keep it, but I am so happy I did (right). It is a real work of art and the colour of the birch branches works well in the moody blue room. Cushions in different shades of blue add further layers of interest.

LAYERED DREAMS.

Deep indigo mixed with natural materials and other shades of blue, muddy browns and neutrals creates a soothing bedroom (overleaf). I like the cocooning atmosphere of dark bedrooms, where the colours seem to embrace you. The wall here is painted in Attic II by Little Greene.

LAYERING DENIMS

When you redecorate a room, you can either do a complete makeover in one go, or take it little by little. Everything does not need to be done at once, and some places and colours should be lived with for a while, so you can get a feel for what you want to do with the rest. If you are starting from scratch and want a whole new look, one way of achieving this is to layer different shades of the same colour. This will create a room that feels very comfortable and soothing to be in, as it is all very tonal and there is nothing to arrest or jolt the eye. Any dark shade of blue will do the trick, as it is very calming and tranquil, whether you choose an intense, rich indigo or a more washed-out denim blue.

NATURALLY DYED

A few months ago, I received an email from South African textile designer Ira Bekker, who wanted to show me her eco-printed linen fabrics. I realized from her description that I would love them. Months passed, and I was lucky enough to be doing a job in Cape Town, so I contacted Ira and she kindly offered to send me a few samples. I was so excited when the package arrived, and when I opened it I fell in love with these masterpieces at first sight and couldn't wait to feature them in some pictures in this book. I love the colour, texture and imperfection of these pieces of fabric with their torn and frayed edges. They work brilliantly as artworks on the wall, or as tablecloths, throws or cushion covers.

'It is an exquisite, alchemical process, filled with beautiful fragrances and magic, in which I am the co-creator, always in awe of the results, which are always surprising and seldom repeated.' – Ira Bekker

MADE BY HAND.

I asked Ira to describe in her own words how these fabrics are made: 'I developed my own style of botanical printing right from the start. Using mostly cottons and linens, I seek out tannin-rich plants, which I lay out onto the fabric then roll it into bundles. Next, I soak the bundles in 'iron juice' for a couple of hours and then either boil or steam the bundles to release the juices from the plant, transferring their colours and textures onto the fabric. It is an exquisite, alchemical process, filled with beautiful fragrances and magic, in which I am the co-creator, always in awe of the results, which are always surprising and seldom repeated'.

CLAY, EARTH & MUD

When I was a boy, my first bedroom was brown, both the furniture and the walls, which were covered with a textural, woven wallpaper. I loved that room and spent so much time in it when I was very young; it was my retreat. I'm not sure whether that was due to the décor or just because I liked hanging out in my own space, but it was a very restful environment. I don't know if my parents were especially interested in colours, but it was the 1970s and shades of brown were very 'in'. Who knows whether it was my choice or theirs, but today brown is one of my favourite colours and I still find that muddy, earthy shades have a very calming effect on me.

HANDMADE.

It was love at first sight when I found these handmade copper tiles (opposite) while I was looking for inspiration for a photoshoot. Their uneven surface gives them a vintage feel, but they look completely up to date when used alongside this concrete bathtub. Their soft gold tones and subtle sheen work very well if you want to warm up a very modern or stark environment. Nature is a rich source of inspiration for muddy colours, especially autumn and winter landscapes. Sculptural dried branches and flowers look beautiful used in still-life displays (left).

PATCHED UP.

To demonstrate how well muddy brown shades can work together, I painted large pieces of canvas in Dark Cocoa Claypaint by Earthborn, and Mahogany and Mouse's Back by Farrow & Ball, then stitched them together to create an oversized patchwork (previous spread). I nailed the finished item to a wall in our summerhouse and we have left it in place, as it makes the perfect backdrop to the antique workbench that houses various books and decorative items.

TONAL DISPLAYS.

Making displays using objects gathered together to tell a story, or just to create interesting juxtapositions, gives a focal point to any space. To make a tonal display, use items in shades of the same colour, with different textures to give a tactile feeling. Arrange small objects on a table, or hang a branch or narrow plank of wood with ropes attached to the ceiling to display fabrics or clothes. The wall is painted in Chocolat by Flamant.

THUNDER, CHARCOAL & NIGHT

Even though I don't like rainy days, I love it when dark, thundery rainclouds roll in. Their moody tones are astoundingly beautiful and every other hue sits so well against them, especially the bright green of spring leaves, which is surely the most beautiful juxtaposition. While you may be reluctant to repaint a room pitch black, I am sure you would be pleasantly surprised if you did, as it is such a chic, comfortable colour to live with. If painting a whole room seems too much, start with one wall or the ceiling. You will see how it grounds the space and sets off any other tint you pair with it. Next time there's a storm, reflect on how beautifully colours pop against the thunder-grey sky.

FOCAL POINT.

A dark colour makes an amazingly atmospheric foundation for any room. The panelled wall (opposite) adds extra texture and movement to the black paint, as the light hitting it creates different shades. Natural materials, such as wood or a large branch with green leaves that stand out dramatically against the backdrop, make great additions. You can pair black or thunder grey with other shades of grey or white for a monochrome look, but they also team easily with any other colour, from yellow or green to red or blue.

CREATE YOUR OWN.

To make a tonal wall, start by painting one solid colour of matt paint in a dark colour and then, using a sponge, apply a wash of diluted lighter paint over it. You might have to repeat this a few times to achieve an effect you are happy with. Testing different colour swatches (opposite) is both fun and interesting, as you might end up choosing an unexpected shade. This picture was shot at the home of the paint company Bauwerk Colour, where they try different shades every day until they find the perfect colour.

CONTRAST.

A dark backdrop will make any other colour stand out beautifully, whether it is a single flower or a piece of furniture, and introducing vibrant colours will instantly brighten a room with dark walls (overleaf). If you are not sure how to get the right look, the best tip I can give is to keep on trying new things and don't be afraid to experiment. It's the best way to find a result that you'll love.

DRAMATIC BACKDROPS

You may think that dark walls would soak up all the light coming into your home and this is partly true, but they also create an unexpected drama that gives a room great interest – and you might be surprised to find that they don't actually make your home feel oppressive and dark. The trick is to add texture and splashes of colour that will lift the effect and ensure that your furniture and collections take centre stage. Think of your home like a theatre, where there always is a focal point that the director draws our attention to, and the set is designed so that nothing distracts us from the main characters and the story being told. Consider your home in the same way, and see where you can create drama with contrasting pieces and by playing with light and shadow.

CENTRE STAGE.

These images show how to add drama to a dark backdrop by using sculptural pieces, such as a simple branch, green leaves or plants, or by playing with contrasting colours to lift the darker surroundings and draw all the attention to the details featured, making them stand out against the solid, dark wall. They also illustrate the power of light, as the objects are softly illuminated while the shadows create intrigue and drama, encouraging the eye to discover new things hiding in the corners as the light changes.

CREATE YOUR OWN MASTERPIECE.

Think of the beautiful paintings of the Dutch Golden Age in the 1600s, when artists painted with such sensibility, highlighting the focal point in their artworks by surrounding the central motif with a darker background to draw attention to it. The way the Dutch masters depicted light and played with contrast, light and shadow is so breathtaking that you can barely take your eyes off their work. You can create a similar effect in your home by, for example, displaying a large branch of spring blossoms or hanging sculptural tulips against a wall on lengths of string. Even a simple still life on a chair can do the trick; well-considered lighting will emphasize the colour, shape and texture and make your still life look like a masterpiece. You can also create a kitchen still life using vegetables or fruit. I love the colour of these lychees against the grey-blue tones of the matt wall, painted in Railings by Farrow & Ball (overleaf). This could have been painted by a Dutch master, don't you agree?

CONTRASTING COLOURS

If you don't want an all-dark interior, you can still create drama by using contrasting colours. Placing dark pieces of furniture and textiles against a lighter backdrop can be just as effective and arresting as when the walls are dark too, as the objects will be thrown into relief. Introducing some elements of natural wood will bring warmth and texture to a scheme that may otherwise seem stark. I always try to soften up interiors by adding a few vintage pieces, as I find that an all-new, shiny interior can lack soul and personality. I tend to work with fabrics and upholstery that have a lot of texture and that are slightly wrinkled, as they add a touch of imperfection, as well as giving more life to the interior and capturing the light in an attractive way.

Adding textural wood and vintage pieces brings warmth and interest to a contrasting interior, which may otherwise feel stark and uninviting.

SOFT FOCUS.

I love a sofa with a linen loose cover that has not been ironed after the last wash. Piled high with soft cushions, it looks so inviting and cosy that you instantly want to curl up on it and relax. The same goes for bed linen, which I think is always best when it is just washed and tumble-dried, as this gives it the perfect texture and softness you need to make your bed feel very comfortable. So, no more ironing needed to get the perfect relaxed look in your home.

down pipe

railings

pitch black

FAVOURITE DYE.

I have a soft spot for grey-dyed linens, and these dye colours, opposite, were a near-perfect match with some of my favourite Farrow & Ball colours: Down Pipe, Railings and Pitch Black. This daybed in our summerhouse is layered with soft linen cushions and thicker linen throws, making it a favourite place to relax or read a book. The fabric wall hanging and large bundle of branches add further layers of texture.

FOREST, MOSS & PINE

I can only guess that my love for dark green pigments stems from being brought up close to a deep forest, which was full of moss and pine trees. It was not a favourite place of mine when I was young, though; then, I only wished to explore big cities and couldn't wait to get away from the forest. But now, years later, when I am living in a large city, I have come to realize how relaxing it is to spend time in the forest of my childhood. The dense colours, the silence and all the different shades of green that nature has to offer are very soothing to the eye. When I visit spaces decorated in a dark green palette, it immediately conjures up that sense of silence and tranquillity.

DIFFERENT SHADES.

There is a vast selection of different shades of green – from the deep, rich hue of pine needles, to the lush, velvety tones of moss, to the lighter yellow-greens of almost translucent foliage. Used individually, layered together or combined with contrasting colours, these shades create very inviting interiors. The magnificent wallpaper (opposite) was designed by RAW Milano for Wall & Decò and is a true piece of art. The layers of different greens and the vintage-style motifs make it a great focal point in any room.

BED OF MOSS.

Aren't we all tempted, when we walk through a forest, to just lie down on a soft bed of moss? I certainly am, and I do so quite often, because I love the softness of it under my back as I look up through the tall pine trees to the sky above. You can create a similar feeling in your bedroom by layering your bed with soft-weave linen in different shades of green. The bed linen shown opposite is from the Swedish company Kardelen. The empty picture frames above the bed make an unusual wall display in their own right.

ADDING NATURE

If you don't want to go completely green at home, or repaint your walls, you can easily introduce the colour by bringing in elements of nature. A small or large plant can do the trick, instantly giving your home life and adding a unique texture that nothing else can bring. I surround myself with green plants, as I love that lush green colour in my home. If you have dark walls, the green hues will stand out and seem stronger, whereas if your walls are lighter, the green tones will add depth and mood to your interior. Green plants bring a touch of nature indoors and are important for your wellbeing; some even help to improve the quality of air in your home, while others, such as a scented geranium, will release a subtle, natural scent into your space.

POPS OF VIVID GREEN.

Anyone who has followed me over the years knows that I have a very soft spot for scented geraniums. Our apartment is filled with different varieties and they all grow rather freely and wildly. I prefer to let plants grow wild, as I love the shape they naturally take. They also add splashes of green to our home, which enhances my feeling of wellbeing and makes me happy. A dark backdrop on the walls will make the most of the lush green tones of house plants and will really ensure the vivid colours pop.

I love white bed linen and don't think there is anything nicer than getting into a bed made with clean, white, linen sheets, softly wrinkled and with that wonderful, newly washed scent. Layering vintage French linen sheets with new, crisp white ones makes it even more inviting, with the different textures and weaves. The metal daybed pictured opposite is in one of my favourite corners in our house in the south of France. I simply nailed a soft vintage linen sheet to the wall behind it to add another layer of texture, while a dried branch makes a raw, natural statement.

White is the first choice for many when it comes to choosing colours for their home. In Sweden, where I am from, it is certainly the preferred colour for walls, and often for furniture, too. I have a conflicting relationship with all-white interiors: I love their fresh, pure look, but at the same time they can feel a little boring and safe. To create a successful pale interior, it is important to work with layers of different textures and the lighter shades of various pigments, and to add vintage surfaces into the mix. On the following pages I have featured interiors where the light palette ranges from pure white to cooler greyish tints mixed with the pale shades of warmer hues.

PALE

PALE INSPIRATIONS

It is not hard to find inspiration from nature in the pale colour range, as the natural landscapes all around us are full of light hues and pigments. Many of these appear in the summer months, when tall grasses along the roadsides have been bleached by the hot sun and lack of rain, and pearlescent shells can be found during walks on the beach. I especially love collecting dried flowers and foliage, wild grasses, and shells and pebbles when I visit the beach. The pale tones of these weathered natural objects add just the right note of interest, warmth and organic texture to an interior that might otherwise seem rather bland and uninteresting. Natural pale colours can, of course, also be found in the winter, when the ground is covered by newly fallen snow, which is so pure and beautiful, and the branches of the trees are covered in a layer of sparkling frost.

The pale tones and organic textures of sun-faded or weathered natural objects, such as dried flowers and shells, add just the right note of interest and warmth to an interior that might otherwise seem rather bland and uninteresting.

COLLECTED IN NATURE.

It is very rare that I come home from our daily early morning or early evening walks during the summer at our house in the south of France without something that has caught my eye. As the summers there are usually hot and arid, many plants and flowers dry out and take on the most beautiful colours and shapes. I particularly love dried-out onion flowers, which grow wild in the ditches, with their sculptural stems that curl and swirl. Other favourites are all the varieties of tall grasses, which dry out in the wind. I rarely go to the beach in the summer, but I love to go out of season to pick up any remaining shells that have not been collected during the summer months.

IVORY, STRING & PARCHMENT

The warmer tones of the pale colour range work very well as part of a pure white scheme, as they add layers of soft, natural warmth that prevent a room from seeming too cold. When it comes to furnishing a pale interior in soft, warm whites, I use unbleached linens to upholster large pieces of furniture, and find that distressed white-painted pieces add a great layer of texture, especially against pristine white walls. I always prefer antique and vintage furniture to newly painted pieces, as the natural imperfections that occur over time are hard to fabricate. Decorative items and collectables in different shades of warm white inspired by nature will add further texture and interest.

WARMER HUES.

These are some of my favourite objects that I have collected over the years on my travels and at various flea markets. Some of them I bought simply because I found them appealing, while others were sourced as props for photoshoots. I love creating displays at home, as it is an easy way to change the look of a room and introduce different textures and colours. The sticks (above) are painted in the following colours: All White from Farrow & Ball, Gauze Mid, Gauze and French Grey Mid from Little Greene.

I love creating little displays at home, as it is a great way to appreciate all the eclectic items I have collected and an easy way to introduce a new look to a room. I especially love the different tones and timeworn texture of vintage white china.

VINTAGE TEXTURES.

I often can't give a reason why I have collected some of the items that fill my tabletops and cabinets. One of these 'for no reason' things I collect is vintage plain white china. I can't say whether it was the shape, colour or function that drew me to each piece, but I truly like them all and use them every day.

ADDING SOFTNESS

Working with textiles will soften the look and feel of any part of your home. They are extremely versatile and can add an extra dimension and sense of movement to a room, which may feel flat and plain in their absence. Personally, I love layering textiles in many different ways. Perhaps the easiest is to add a throw and extra cushions to your sofa or bed, creating softness and comfort but at the same time adding different weaves or colours. Another way of introducing more fabrics into everyday life is to use a tablecloth and soft linen napkins when setting the table for breakfast, lunch or dinner – there's no need to wait for a special occasion, as using a cloth will make every meal feel special. Replacing your wardrobe doors with a curtain, or using a piece of fabric to cover an open shelf, are other great tricks to add a soft touch to your home.

OPENED OR CLOSED.

Clothes can be stored in an ordinary wardrobe,
but another option is to use clothes rails with
panels of fabric hanging from curtain poles
attached to the ceiling to screen them off. Linen
is the best choice, as it only needs to be washed
and tumble-dried before you hang it up again. You
could even make your own clothes rail using fairly
straight tree branches, with part of the smaller
branches kept intact to hang your clothes from.
You can either paint the branches, as I have here,
or keep them natural, depending on the look you
prefer. Either way, you would have a good-value,
useful storage unit for everyday clothes, which
would work equally well in a bedroom or hallway.

1 ROTTBOLLIA HIRSUTA.

SOFTER LAYERS.

If you have plain white walls, I strongly suggest adding some layers of texture and introducing different shades of soft white to make your room feel more inviting. In a bedroom, this can easily be done by using bed linen dyed in various pale shades and tones of white. In our summerhouse (opposite), I draped the frame of the four-poster bed with linen sheets to create a warm and cosy feel. Another way of bringing texture and interest to a plain white room is to use vintage pieces of furniture as shown above, where the distressed white-painted metal furniture, the aged mirror and the collection of accessories add texture and interest. If you have a limited amount of desk space, one way of providing storage is to suspend wire baskets from a rope attached to the wall or ceiling. The vintage etching, string of shells and vintage fabric flowers (above right and right) are part of my own collection, as I like their textures and pale tones.

VINTAGE CONTRAST.

A wall displaying a collection of mirrors (opposite) is a brilliant idea for adding both texture and an original form of decoration to an interior. The frames of the mirrors add their various patinas to the textural palette, while the mirrors themselves reflect and accentuate any light in the room. This is a particularly effective solution for a small space that has a limited amount of natural light, as the mirrors will magnify its effect and make the room feel larger. A simple piece of fabric stitched onto a rope is a clever and unusual way to hide open shelves and keep them dust-free (this page).

SWEDISH HERITAGE

I have a real soft spot for Swedish furniture and objects dating from around the seventeenth century. I love the simplicity of the pieces, but also the colours they are painted in, which range from soft, warm white to pale grey. The unique patina, formed through years of use, is just extraordinary and brings great character to any up-to-date interior. You can use antique Swedish furniture to make a statement as a standalone piece or gathered together as part of a collection, but it also works just as well mixed in with modern items. I tend to look out for original pieces where the paintwork is intact, even if it is very worn and scraped; I would never repaint a piece, as this would decrease its value and it would lose its original beauty. Such furniture can be on the expensive side, but I think it is worthwhile saving up to buy a real antique instead of settling for something newly produced. You will be able to cherish a piece of furniture like this forever.

MEMORIES.
I was kindly allowed to shoot these pictures at an antique dealer's place in the village where my mother's side of the family is from and where I spent a lot of my childhood with my grandparents. The antique dealer's showroom is in an old furniture factory, which has now moved on to new premises. Some of my family used to work in the factory and I enjoyed hanging out there during my childhood, especially as I loved the smell of freshly cut wood.

Antique Swedish furniture works well as a standalone piece, as part of a collection or mixed in with modern items. Its unique patina, formed through years of use, is just extraordinary, and I love the character and texture it brings to any up-to-date interior.

STYLE.

A friend remarked that she doesn't think my style is typically Swedish, and she asked me where the way I style my home and photos comes from. I couldn't give her an answer, having never really thought about it. I consider my style to be quite Scandinavian, but I guess it depends on where you are from and how you see things. Featured here is a corner of our flat in Paris, where I love the juxtaposition of the Swedish antique chair with the French ornamental fireplace and gilt mirror. The vintage chest and gilt-framed painting (opposite) are another very simple yet eye-catching combination.

WALL ART.
One thing I find hard when it comes to decorating my own home is hanging wall art. It seems so permanent, as it normally involves drilling a hole, but why that should be so difficult, I don't know! So a lot of my walls are empty. It's not a big deal really, but I do love decorated walls. A great way of adorning a wall is to hang vintage textiles instead of pictures. I bought the one shown here at a flea market in the south of France and I love everything about it.

WASHED, BLEACHED & WEATHERED

There is nothing like the faded colours of washed vintage French linen, smooth driftwood or antique grey-painted furniture, and I love everything about these soft, warm tones. I am always collecting pieces of wood from the beach and the forest; I use some to light the fire, but the sculptural pieces usually end up on display. They have the same undertone as the wooden floorboards you find in very old houses, where the planks have taken on the softest hue and texture from years of wear and exposure to light. Wood that has weathered with time and use has a colour and patina that is hard to replicate, so I am always on the lookout for such objects or furniture.

COLLECTING.

I'm a true collector. Some of the things I collect might seem meaningless, but to me they are treasures. It could be a particular shape or colour that first catches my eye, then once I have lived with a piece for a while and it has a special place at home, it feels like it is part of the story. Some examples are the beautiful stack of empty boxes (far left), a bundle of dried lavender (left) and some pieces of wood found on a walk in the countryside (opposite).

SOFT TO TOUCH.

I can't tell you how many vintage French linen sheets I own,
but I can promise you there are a good few piles of them.
I must admit that I don't use them all, but to me they look
beautiful just piled up, such as the collection shown opposite,
which features a mix of vintage and new linens with fabulous
textures and colours. It is rare to find linen sheets of such good
quality today, so I can't resist buying them when I see them.
They are very useful, as they can be cut up to make scatter
cushions, a loose cover for a worn upholstered chair, curtains
or even substitute wardrobe 'doors', as featured on page 66.
I also like beds to be layered with a lot of pillows, which
are comfortable to lean against when reading a book or just
relaxing. I particularly love the effect of a heavy-weave linen
used as a bedcover combined with new, subtly embroidered
cushions (this page).

I have a vast collection of vintage French linen sheets, which I love for their soft, tactile texture and subtle colour tones. I think they look beautiful stacked in piles on shelves or chairs, layered on beds, or made into cushions, curtains or loose covers.

HARMONIOUS CONTRAST

Combining a range of shades from the same colour base can give a very successful result, as it ensures that all the elements sit together harmoniously and create a layered tonal look with more depth than a single-colour scheme. I am all for adding texture to an interior, but this doesn't mean using only vintage pieces, as lots of new furniture and decorative items have beautiful textures and colouring. I like to mix new with old, shiny with matt, rough with smooth, as it is always the contrast or the layering that interests the eye. When I work on styling jobs, I invariably find that contrast is what makes the picture. For example, if you have super-modern furniture against a super-modern background, it can look quite soulless, but if you set the modern furniture against an older, scruffier background, it immediately becomes interesting, as the contrasting elements lift each other and bring the interior to life.

SHADES OF PALE.

This desk space (opposite) demonstrates the inviting effect that can be created by using a palette that combines different paler shades. Pure white has been layered with softer, warmer tones, but I also added in some cooler shades to show how well they work together, resulting in a setting that is so comfortable to live with. It has all the elements I think an interior needs – a mix of vintage and new, textural wood playing off shiny porcelain, and a collection of favourite tonal objects gathered together. The distressed painted wood chair (below right) exhibits a wonderful array of different pale hues, ranging from warm to cool.

ADDING GREEN.

A key element to add to any interior or picture is something green. If you look at a room and feel that something is missing, but you can't put your finger on what it is, try introducing some greenery. It can be a single leaf, a potted plant or a few stems of wild onion flowers, as I have used here in this simple glass jar. It is a trick I often use, especially if a picture or room set doesn't feel right, and almost every time it proves to be the last extra touch that is needed.

LOOSE COVERED.

One of the most practical solutions for upholstered furniture is covering it with loose covers/slipcovers. They are easy to remove and wash, and it gives the piece a relaxed look, in keeping with the not-too-perfect feel that I often try to achieve. My goal is always to try to create an interior that has a lived-in vibe. In my own home, I don't mind if things get a bit crooked or wrinkled, as it is part and parcel of everyday life, and there are so many more important things to worry about than a pristine interior. Above all, a home is, and should always be, for living in.

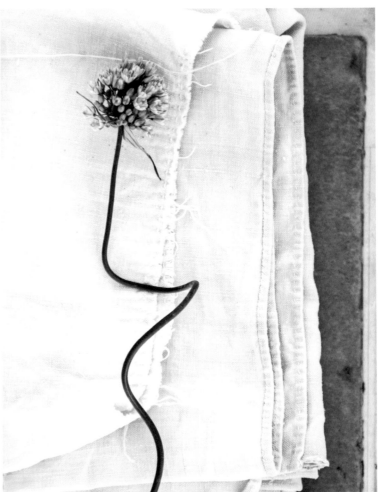

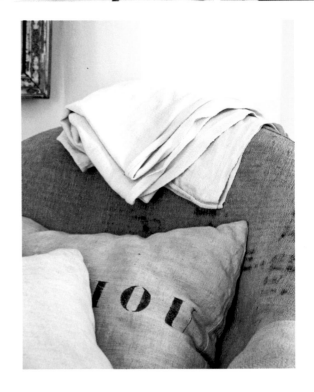

ADDING TEXTURE.

Creating a textural mix in an all-white room will give it more depth and interest, as the different materials bring an extra dimension to an otherwise plain look. There is nothing wrong with plain, but if you want to add something extra, items with a rich patina will help you to create a multi-layered effect. I love mirrors, both for their decorative quality and because they reflect light and add depth to any room. Antique French mirrors, such as the ones shown opposite, are easy to find at flea markets in most countries, and displaying several together on one wall makes an eye-catching statement. The chaise longue is a vintage French one with a new patched-up cover made out of vintage food bags. The lampshade was home-made from a heavy-weave fabric painted with regular emulsion. Distressed paintwork has a lovely texture (above left), so I always advise against repainting worn vintage furniture, as it can lose its charm. Layering cushions and throws onto any piece of upholstered furniture will instantly make it more inviting (right).

ICE, CLOUD & SNOW

Even though I am not a winter person, there is something magical about newly fallen snow, when the ground is covered in the purest of white, which reflects light and absorbs noise, making everything seem so quite and still. In Sweden, where I grew up, we sometimes had incredibly beautiful winter days, with clear blue sky and everything covered in frost that sparkled like a scattering of crystals. When it comes to pure white interiors, it is important to add some tactile layers so the result doesn't feel stark or cold. Working with a mix of materials in different shades of white will bring warmth and comfort to rooms that take their inspiration from snowy landscapes.

WHITE ON WHITE.
The picture opposite was taken in photographer Debi Treloar's house, where she kindly allowed me to paint her (formerly red!) Chesterfield sofa pure white, using regular matt emulsion. I love the result – it looks like a big puffy cloud! You can never go wrong if you set a table with a selection of all-white china (left). Simply add some soft table linen, food and freshly picked flowers, and you will have a quick and easy table setting that is very welcoming and pleasing to the eye.

CRISP WHITE LINEN

Food always looks the most appetizing to me when it is served on white china plates with white table linen. This is by no means a rule, and it might seem boring to some, but I think it always makes every meal look fresh and tasty. I can't resist all-white vintage china, especially any that comes from former restaurants, as it is usually very good quality and I love the thickness of the porcelain. This type of tableware, layered with a linen tablecloth and napkins, makes for a simple yet stunning table setting. The various pieces of china and textiles will never be the exact same shade of white, so your table will naturally feature varying tones and textures. If you prefer new table linen, good-quality linen cloths can be sourced from many mainstream brands, but great vintage ones can still be found at flea markets.

RECIPE WALL.

A simple way to add texture to a plain kitchen wall – while providing inspiration for your next meal – is to stick up your favourite recipes torn from a book or magazine. For easy-grab kitchen towels and cloths, hang them on a branch suspended on ropes from the ceiling. This is a great way to create easy-to-reach storage, and can also be used for kitchen utensils hung on S-shaped hooks. The chairs belonged to my grandmother and I use them every day, either for sitting on or as extra storage.

PERFECT PLACE.

A lounge area beside a large window overlooking the garden is something that can be used every day. This daybed, designed by Debi Treloar, was made from simple wooden planks, painted pure white to blend into the surrounding white space. The raised back and one side mean that it can function as a sofa as well as a bed, while the high back also doubles as a shelf. Layered with simple linen sheets and soft cushions, it is a place for relaxing, where you could easily stay for hours looking out at the ever-changing natural world.

One of my favourite things to collect is plain white china, both new and old, but especially any that has come from former restaurants, as I love the thickness of the porcelain. This utilitarian china is normally really good quality and will last a lifetime.

RARE LUXURY.
This picture was captured during one of our breakfasts at home. I couldn't resist photographing the setting as I just thought it looked too inviting not to share with you. We don't get to do this very often as we travel a lot, but when we are at home we always try to make every moment special, particularly when it comes to eating, when we like to make the effort to create a mood of luxury and indulgence. The china and linens are a mix of new and vintage, and I find the different qualities and shades of white mixed together very pleasing.

REARRANGE.

Our home is always changing. Furniture gets moved around, cushions are given new covers, newly bought props are added, and new 'spaces within the space' are created. I find it very inspiring to make some changes from time to time, as it makes a room feel new and different. I know some spaces are not that easy to rearrange, but it is worth a try, as it is a very inexpensive way to create a new look at home. When things start to seem a little stale and you feel like a change, the easy thing to do is to run out and buy something new, but that is not always necessary – a simple re-shuffle can do the trick.

PIGMENTS.

While creating this book, we had the opportunity to photograph a summerhouse belonging to the owners of lime paint company Bauwerk Colour in Germany. It was full of colour pigments, colour swatches and painted swatches on the walls; the whole place just breathed colour and was so inspiring. This vintage workbench was covered with old glass bottles filled with different shades of natural colours. I would recreate this look at home in an instant if I had the space (and time), as it makes such a beautiful still life, whether you are planning to mix colours or not.

Every colour on this planet is inspired by nature, but what we typically think of as 'natural' tones are the shades of greens, browns, taupes, soft blues and greys associated with the landscape. I have a huge crush on these colours, which seem to be lifted straight from nature. The colours in the natural palette range from the pale green of olive leaves to deeper shades of hazelnut and wood, but also include the brighter, spring-like tones inspired by apples, figs and fresh new leaves. Natural colours work well on their own, mixed together or added into any other colour scheme. These are versatile hues that are easy to work with and will bring a natural feeling to your home.

NATURAL

NATURAL INSPIRATIONS

All the things I love in nature offer the perfect inspiration for a natural colour range. Wherever your eyes rest in the ever-changing environment, you will see shades that will, without hesitation, fit into a natural scheme. I guess this is one of the reasons I love nature, as it is just there, all around us, and all we have to do is keep our eyes wide open and take it all in. Even though sometimes there is too much beauty to absorb all at once, our brain is clever enough to remember the parts we really love. Whatever kind of landscape I'm surrounded by, I can't take my eyes off it, and my pockets and hands are always full of natural finds wherever I go. There is as much inspiration to be found in a dry desert as in a lush forest, and they both deliver such a different range of natural colours, with none being any more beautiful than the other.

I love nature, as it is just there, all around us, without us even having to look, and all we have to do is keep our eyes wide open and take it all in, even though sometimes there is too much beauty to memorize it all.

NATURAL BEAUTY.

It's all too easy to overlook the beauties of nature, as we sometimes don't take the time to stop, reflect and really look. When I do, I always find new things to inspire me. Any sculptural branch with dried leaves, berries or seeds is beautiful when brought home and put on display. I also love to collect feathers, as every one is unique, and they make a charming wall decoration. Fruits, nuts and vegetables are always in the right range of tones to work as part of a natural colour scheme, like these beautiful raw green almonds and the dried-out corn shown above.

NATURALLY SET.

Create a natural table setting using wooden plates, soft linens and vintage newspapers as placemats. Add natural colours by painting wooden cutlery in soft shades, such as Sage Green, Bone China Blue and Pearl Colour from Little Greene.

HAZELNUT, TERRACOTTA & WOOD

The deeper shades of the natural colour spectrum are inspired by autumnal pigments and objects darkened by time and use. The colours range from the rich golden hue of hazelnuts to the darker tones of terracotta and cut wood that has been left out to weather. All of these colours have a soft feel and are easy to use in any style of interior, whether you introduce them in the form of furniture and objects or decide to repaint your walls. These darker shades work really well mixed in with the lighter and brighter range of natural pigments, as they complement each other beautifully. Vintage wooden and rattan furniture are key elements to incorporate when creating this look.

NATURALLY WARM.

All of the inspirations shown here will bring a mellow softness to the home. The tones of the hazelnuts (above) range from gold to deep brown and work well in this colour scheme. Stacked wood (far left) adds texture and a living material to the home, while terracotta pots (left) bring a touch of warmth; over time, they will develop a fantastic patina, so don't scrub them clean. A stack of vintage rattan trunks and baskets (opposite) adds natural colour and texture, and can be used for storage or as side tables.

NATURAL FOCUS.

Combining textural layers of wood, natural linen, string and dried branches never goes wrong (this page) – it is one of the easiest and least expensive ways to add a natural warmth to your home. The doors and doorframes shown opposite have been painted many times over the years, but have now been stripped to reveal the wood beneath. The layers of paint have protected the wood and given it a soft, natural hue that blends in with the pale surrounding walls. The chances are, if you start scraping old paint off joinery or wooden furniture, you will reveal the beautiful patina of the wood underneath and you won't ever want to repaint it. If you are lucky enough to have anything like this at home, my advice is to leave it as it is.

WOODEN TEXTURES

Adding natural elements and tones into an otherwise light colour scheme will warm up an interior and give it an organic edge. Raw, untreated wood will work in any style of home. I prefer the look and feel of vintage untreated wood, which has been softened and mellowed over the course of time and through years of handling and use. As a natural material, newly bought untreated wood will stain easily, so you should protect the surface by treating it with oil, which gives a softer, more natural finish than lacquer. You can also add colour pigment to the oil, if you want to give the wood a slight tint. I recommend using a light greyish pigment, which gives the wood a warm grey tone, as though it has aged naturally.

BUILT UP.

I had the idea of using a stack of firewood to make a place to relax when I was looking at some chopped-up logs piled high in our garage one day (opposite). I used a wide plank of wood to create a flat surface that I topped with a mattress and some soft cushions. I just love this extra seating area that was made on the spur of the moment and it has become one of our favourite places to hang out, as the garage is the coolest part of the house during the hot summer. Juniper berries, a small bees' nest and some dried-out artichokes (below) can all be used for colour inspiration or simple decoration.

Sometimes you look at something and see how easily it can be transformed into something else, which is what happened when I created this log sofa. For years, it was a pile of firewood, until one day the idea to make it into a seat suddenly came to me.

OLIVE, CACTUS & SAGE

With some colours it's love at first sight, while others take longer to get used to. One range of colours that I fell for immediately, and for which I've had a soft spot for as long as I can remember, are the soft green tones of olive, cactus and sage. These colours are hard to describe, as they can be so changeable due to light or shade, looking quite green in some lights and distinctly grey with only a hint of green in others. This characteristic makes it an interesting colour range to work with, as the effect will vary dramatically depending on the quality of the light. Maybe that is why I like this colour palette so much, as it is so versatile and always a bit different.

SOME FAVOURITE INSPIRATIONS.
Three of my favourites: olive (above), sage (far left) and cactus (left). Olive trees have amazing two-tone leaves with a darker shade on top and a silvery green underside. I love watching them move in the wind, as there is a magical reflective effect when the silvery sides catch the light. Sage also has soft, silvery leaves that become two-tone when dried. Cacti are a favourite plant of mine. The fleshy leaves beneath the prickles are so smooth and I find their blue-green shade soothing.

TONAL.

Layering colours within the same scheme will give your room a muted, calm look, and at the same time add interest. The most common way to create two-tone walls is to paint a darker colour on the lower part of the wall and a lighter one above, but we did it the other way round here (opposite), using Steel and Day by Bauwerk Colour, and I think it works just as well. You can also add tonal interest by painting a large canvas with lime paint (this page). It looks like an expensive artwork but is very easy to do and a great way to add more colour to your home. This canvas is painted in Tumble by Hans Blomquist for Bauwerk Colour and the wall behind is Milkweed by Bauwerk Colour.

PAINTED BY NATURE

Some of nature's colour combinations are just so beautiful that they stop me in my tracks. Natural colour schemes always have a depth and softness to them and feel so unmanufactured that if you decide to redecorate your home in any of these shades, they will give it a real sense of integrity. In my view, any colour that is earthy or has a soft green tint will work in any style of home, both as a base colour and as an accent. You can never go wrong if you choose any shade that is inspired by the natural range of colours, as they will make your home feel warm, inviting and relaxing.

BREATHTAKING.

I stumbled across these pheasant's eggs when I was propping for a job in London. I was on the hunt for pale-coloured eggs in pastel blue, pink and beige. But then I saw boxes of pheasant eggs and couldn't believe how beautiful they were, in shades ranging from dark brown to soft beige and khaki. I bought a few boxes so I could feature them in this book – they were just too stunning not to share!

Natural colour schemes have a depth and softness to them, and feel so unmanufactured and true in their shades that they will always bring a sense of integrity to your home and make it feel warm, inviting and relaxing.

NATURALLY SOFT.

These stunning rooms are in the home of
the founders of the Bauwerk Colour paint
company. Photographer Debi and I knew
it was going to be something special as
we drove up to the front door. We couldn't
wait to get inside and when we did, as you
can guess, we absolutely fell in love with
it. The interior has not been renovated for
many years, and it was so full of beauty and
texture that it was hard to know where to
start or what to photograph, as we wanted
to capture it all (you will find a lot of pictures
of this amazing house throughout the book).
I love the gentle tones and the spontaneous
decoration of the rooms. The deep windows
filter the light so beautifully that it gives the
interior a very dreamy feeling.

SPRING, FIG & APPLE

The brighter hues of the natural colour range are inspired by figs, apples and the light green of fresh new leaves when they first unfurl on the trees. When compared to the other colours in the natural range, this lush palette is the most vibrant. These brighter shades of green work very well as accent colours and will add an uplifting pop to any interior, whether the foundation of the scheme is light or dark. Painting an entire room in bright colours, however, can feel quite invasive and often overwhelms everything else in the room, so start by adding some bright-coloured furniture or accessories, or paint just one wall to create a focal point.

ANYTHING GOES.

There are many bright greens to be inspired by, especially in the spring, as the first leaves, grasses and fruits slowly start to appear, with their vibrant but soft hues. I love it when the trees begin to unfurl their leaves and gradually burst into life. These sweet chestnut (*Castanea sativa*) leaves are so lush and beautiful, with their fluffy seed cases just starting to form (opposite). Other bright green inspirations are leafy, aromatic fig branches (far left), the first figs (left) and onions (above).

READY TO MIX.

It is so amazing to watch an expert mixing colours and creating a new paint shade. The company Bauwerk Colour, in whose studio this picture was taken, mixes colours all the time and it is fascinating to see how, by adding less or more of, for example, black, the resulting colour becomes so different. It is a work of art. At the time of writing, I am also working on my own paint range for Bauwerk Colour, so I will soon head to their home again, to start mixing my colour range with them. It is such an exciting project and I can't wait to see these new colours taking shape.

TONAL LAYERING

As I have already mentioned, I think that adding touches of green to your home – whether in the form of plants, furniture or accessories – makes any room come to life. Mixing different green hues together and introducing them as colour accents in either a dark or light interior will give equally beautiful results. Combining the more muted range of green shades with either bright or soft pastels will look very natural and will give you a subtle, tonal display. Working with the same colour base but mixing darker tones with the lighter shades achieves a very textural look with great depth, but it also gives a multicoloured effect, even though the shades are all from the same colour range.

Green is an uplifting, natural addition to any room or colour scheme. Brighter green hues work very well as accent colours in the home and will add a vibrant pop to any kind of interior, whether the base colours are light or dark.

GREEN MIX.

The mix of green colours in the picture opposite greatly pleases me. The dark green vintage chest of drawers works beautifully with the lighter, pastel green of the old metal container and the deep, fresh green of the leaves on the chestnut branches. Touches of gold bring another layer to the otherwise tonal display. An old window and a panel of vintage wallpaper (below left) work well as wall art, while also breaking up the pure white wall and creating a focal point on the white chest of drawers. A collection of vintage green glass vases (below right) would look as good grouped together on a table or mantelpiece as they do on this chest.

ADDING POPS OF GREEN

The easiest way to bring green into your home is to add pot plants, foliage or large, leafy branches. I wish everyone could add flowers to their home every week, as floral arrangements are so eye-catching in any room, either as a centrepiece on the kitchen table or on a side table. You don't have to spend a lot of money, however, as there are lots of common shrubs, bushes or trees that you can cut a leafy branch off on a walk in the countryside – but please use secateurs for a clean, damage-free cut. If you want more colour, a floral arrangement will do the trick, and what is more beautiful than a bouquet of garden flowers? Nature is not only one of the key ingredients in any interior, but it is also one of the easiest ways to add colour to your space.

NATURALLY ADDED.

Even the smallest of green additions can do the trick. A simple glass with a sprig of clover or a flower can be all that is needed (above right), while the texture and vibrant colour of the seedheads make a dramatic contrast with vintage linen fabric (above left). This rustic trestle is a great surface for a natural display, with a vintage watering can making a charming substitute for a vase (opposite). A branch from the laden apple tree of our neighbours in the south of France looks striking on a table in a clear glass vase (overleaf).

Decorating with a soft colour scheme will create a dreamy look and introduce colour without being too 'colourful'. Pastel hues can appear childish if they are too pure or baby-like, so choose slightly nondescript colours with a dusty finish. Most colours are more comfortable to live with if they have black in them, as it makes them dirtier and more interesting. A soft palette ranges from dusty pink, to duck-egg blue, to vanilla yellow. These shades work well together, on walls, furniture or as accessories, on either a dark or light base.

SOFT

SOFT INSPIRATIONS

Sourcing soft colours in nature is not as easy as one might imagine. Don't get me wrong, there is a lot of inspiration to be found within this colour range, but it is very much concentrated on flowers, some vegetables, and hen and duck eggs. In one way, this makes me think that soft colours should be used only as accents in the home, as this is how they appear in the natural environment. On the other hand, the soft colours in this range are far too beautiful to use in just small doses, as these gentle hues are very comfortable and soothing to live with. For someone like myself who loves flowers, it is of course easy to find inspiration for many different shades of dusty pink, light blue and soft yellow, but when it comes to sourcing other natural objects it is a little more challenging, as many colours are in the brighter and bolder range.

Dusty, soft colours appear as accents in the natural environment, but these pretty hues are far too beautiful to use only as colour accents in the home. Pale, soft and soothing, they are easy and comfortable to live with and can be enjoyed in a wholehearted manner.

NATURALLY SOFT.

When I started to gather together natural objects to photograph as inspirations for this chapter, I seemed to find nothing but flowers to represent the colours I wanted to feature and it was harder than I thought to find other naturally growing things that illustrated the soft colour range. But, when I started to think laterally, there were many more objects to source, and you will see examples of these soft inspirations throughout this chapter. I don't have a clue what these dried, small pink balls are (far left), but they are so pretty and their colour is so beautiful that I had to include them. Also featured here are soft yellow pears, papery poppies, which come in so many extraordinary colours, and mini-aubergines/eggplants, which have a pale, nearly pistachio hue.

ROSE, POWDER & PETAL

It is strange to think that once, many years ago, it was decided that pink, in any shape or form, was a girly colour, whereas light blue was appropriate for boys. I remember asking my mother to dye a pair of my white trousers pink, as I wanted a pair so badly; of course, she asked me if I was sure. I was, and I went to school the next day thinking I looked really good, but most of my friends didn't agree, so there were a lot of looks and comments. It didn't really matter to me, as I liked them, but it made me realize that certain colours are for certain things. But now is the time to challenge convention and let colours be colours, used by everyone, with no rules or regulations.

LET'S ALL GO PINK.
A large branch laden with cherry blossom makes a stunning addition to any room (opposite). Certain flowers never fail to make me happy when they come into bloom and cherry blossom is one of them, so I always try to bring some home to celebrate the arrival of spring. Soft pink textiles and cushion covers match some of my favourite pink paints: Delicacy from Sanderson and Milk Thistle from Little Greene (above). Vintage roses are favourite flowers of mine, as I love their scent and delicate pink petals (far left).

A SOFT LOOK

Creating a soft and gentle scheme is quite easy, as the different shades in this colour spectrum tend to be harmonious and will give you an up-to-date interior that is comfortable to live in. You can either embrace the look wholeheartedly by choosing furnishings in toning colours, or introduce contrasting darker hues. A gentle scheme is traditionally romantic and can feel quite feminine, but if you accessorize it with contemporary furniture and objects, you can make the look more neutral. Having said that, I prefer not to label colours – or anything else, for that matter – masculine or feminine, as I think we can be more creative than that. We all have the right to choose the colours we love and to furnish our homes with our favourite furniture and accessories.

STYLISHLY SOFT.

Dried flowers are one of the most beautiful things there are. The colours of most blooms become even more stunning when dried and their petals and leaves take on a tactile, paper-like quality. These peonies were just too glorious not to photograph for this book, both for their texture and colour inspiration (below). The romantic room opposite illustrates a perfect soft combination, with the light pink sofa and a duck-egg blue wall that has been painted and patched with roses and leaves. Both inviting and stylish, it would be a successful look to recreate.

SOFT FLORALS.

This is an inviting spot to hang out, where layers of printed textiles are mixed with plain fabrics and pillowcases in soft textures and tones. A few darker colours have been introduced to break up the scheme and give it some depth. The French metal daybed was found at a flea market and the cushions and textiles are a mix of new and vintage. The backdrop has been painted in two tones, using soft Dorchester Pink for the panelling, and mixing it with pale grey Mono for the walls, both from Little Greene.

A soft colour scheme is traditionally romantic and can seem quite feminine, but if you accessorize it with contemporary furniture and objects you can make the look more neutral or masculine.

USING PATTERNS.

I have had a soft spot for floral patterns for as long as I can remember. A traditional choice for country-style interiors, florals are often considered old-fashioned by those who prefer a clean, contemporary look, but for me, floral prints work everywhere and can be incorporated into any look you want. Of course, a soft-looking interior with floral patterns sits very comfortably in a country-esque setting, and maybe that is where it fits best, but I would love to see more creativity than that when it comes to mix and match, and urge you to be adventurous. Layer different kinds of floral patterns, using faded vintage prints and soft linens to create a perfect corner for daydreaming in your city apartment or country house (above right). Another idea is to use vintage maps as wallpaper, or to make a headboard by papering a square the same width as your bed, then dress the bed with soft dyed textiles to add textural layers to your bedroom (above left).

SOFTLY LAYERED.

These images were photographed in fashion designer Marie Sixtine's apartment in Paris. The warm mix of natural wood, painted furniture and soft textiles makes both spaces very inviting, while the layers of textures and the mural painted by Alexandre Poulaillon give them a very personal look. The way the interior is decorated and the combination of soft colours used throughout give it a calming vibe. The space was exceptionally relaxing and comfortable to be in, and all my senses – especially touch and sight – felt instantly soothed.

DUSKY SHADES

Decorating with soft colours that have a dirtier undertone and a dustier finish than the purer pastel shades creates a space in which the colours used seem almost secondary. They become quite nondescript, as they take on a different tone and feel depending on the light in the room – both natural and artificial – and the other colours you choose to include. Dusky colours will also give a moodier look, as they won't make your interior as bright and light as a pure, clean colour would. If you then throw some darker colours into the mix to add depth and contrast, it will give you an up-to-date scheme that will make your home look sophisticated and stylish rather than pale and uninteresting.

ADDING CONTRAST.

Using contrasting colours that share the same undertones will give any space more depth and interest, as the different colours will enhance each other while also working together harmoniously. For instance, if you want to mix a dusty pink with a darker grey, as shown here, you should choose a soft shade of pink with a dusty undertone and a grey paint that has a slightly lilac cast. This room is furnished with vintage furniture with dark upholstery and textiles to contrast with the walls. The window frames have been painted in a dark grey gloss, which contrasts beautifully with the walls and also reflects the light coming in through the large windows.

A combination of soft colours and textures creates a very calm and comfortable environment that is soothing for all the senses, especially touch and sight.

PAINTED BY NATURE.

These rose petals (opposite) have the most delicate, paper-like texture, and the romantic mix of dusty pinks, blackened mauves and pale yellows look beautiful and would make a great colour inspiration for any room. This bouquet of roses and eucalyptus was given to us by a friend who stayed in our flat while we were travelling. We enjoyed it fresh for a couple of days before the next trip, and when we came back, it had completely dried out and looked so stunning, with all the colours working beautifully together.

DECORATED WALLS

There are so many ways to add colour or pattern to your walls, and the easiest one is to paint them any colour you like. Hanging wallpaper requires a little more effort and skill, while adding paintings, framed prints or decorative objects could either prove to be a simple task or take more time, depending on the number and how you choose to hang them. As well as introducing colour to your home, decorating the walls is a great way to express your personality, make a feature of your collections or just create an attractive display. However you decide to do it – even if all you choose to do is refresh them with a new coat of paint in the existing colour – it will be well worth the time it takes. Beautifully decorated walls help to create a homely, warm feeling.

EYE-CATCHING FLORALS.

I struggle with the idea of hanging wallpaper on my walls – I'm always worried I might tire of the pattern quickly and want to change it. However, the wallpaper featured here is a design I really fell for, designed by Ellie Cashman. I adore the large printed flowers and the contrasting black background. Instead of pasting it onto my walls, I came up with the idea of hanging it with large clips. I am now completely in love with this beautiful backdrop, and even more so because it is moveable.

PISTACHIO, DUCK EGG & FADED DENIM

I consider myself a 'blue' person. Denim blue, greyish blue, duck-egg blue, shades of blue that veer towards green and anything in between are all favourites of mine, both to live with and to wear. My wardrobe is full of blue shirts in every shade. It is such a versatile colour because it goes with almost anything, is easy on the eye and comes in so many different tones – although this does make it harder to choose just one, especially when it comes to painting your home. You can rarely go wrong if you decorate with any shade of faded blue or pistachio green, but I do recommend that you choose hues that contain a touch of black pigment, so the result is more 'dusty' than 'baby'.

AMAZING SHADES.

This colour palette encompasses a wonderful range of soft blues and greens. Some great inspirations include hen's eggs (above), in such exquisite shades that they are nearly too beautiful to eat. Painted antique Swedish furniture (far left) illustrates the perfect range of colours, from soft blue-grey to green. Some shirt collars I found at a flea market (left) are just the right washed-out tones. The stunning silk-upholstered antique sofa (opposite) could easily take centre stage in any space.

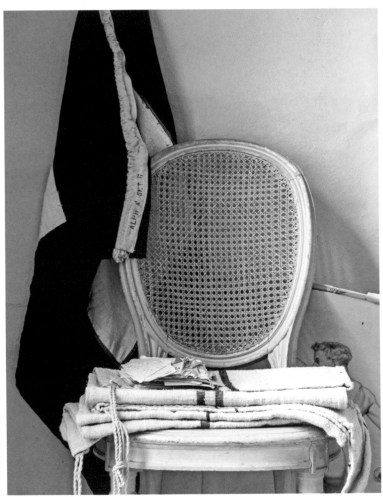

DUCK-EGG BLUE

This is a shade that is so soft and comfortable to live with that it can easily work as a wall colour, on painted furniture or in textiles, in any style of interior. I know I have probably already claimed that other colours are my favourites, and it is so hard to choose only one when the world around us is such a stunning source of colour, spoiling us for choice with so many glorious shades. But if I have to come off the fence, blue is my absolute favourite – dark, light, soft or bold, but always with a dusty feeling due to the addition of black. Duck-egg blue is a soft colour that can be mixed with any other, and that makes it very versatile as a backdrop, as you can add furniture in any other colour you like, from black to white and all shades in between.

It can be hard to find locations that are perfect for the look I want to achieve when creating interiors to photograph. Many homeowners don't allow repainting, so I have had to come up with other ways to show different colours. One solution was to tape painted pieces of paper together to cover a wall (opposite). I discovered this beautiful old painted cabinet (above left) in an antique shop in Sweden. A charming French chair from a flea market (above right) displays my favourite vintage linen sacks.

SOFT SPOT.

It is easy to create an inviting bedroom scheme using shades of duck-egg blue and pistachio green, as these colours have a soothing effect and will make anyone feel calm and relaxed. Darker greys work well with these soft tones, adding depth and making a room feel cosy and intimate. Here, a couple of old metal deed boxes serve as a bedside table. The paper bowls and plates opposite have been painted in a few of my favourite soft blues and greens: Farrow & Ball's Lichen (top right), Teresa's Green (centre) and Parma Grey (below). The white porcelain spoons were bought from Merci in Paris.

FADED DENIMS

Shades of denim can range from the deepest indigo to the palest, soft grey-blue. I love how this versatile fabric changes over many years of being worn and washed, becoming softer and paler but remaining as beautiful as when it was new. If you want to give newly bought cotton and linen pillowcases and other textiles that lovely soft texture and faded colour that come through years of use, I recommend that you wash them over and over again to achieve the desired look. Alternatively, hunt for vintage textiles that already have the right texture and colour. This would always be my preference, but either way, you will create a look that feels warm and inviting, with wonderful faded colours that will sit really well with other soft hues.

SOFT SEATING.
Even now, sitting here writing, I feel an urge to throw myself onto this cushion-filled sofa and stay there for a long time! The different shades of blues and soft greens complement each other beautifully and work well alongside the large antique mirrors and old windows that make this flat (belonging to the owner of Depuis Toujours in the south of France) so inviting and personal. The soft shades of faded vintage paint (below left) and upholstery fabrics (below right) are always very inspirational when searching for the right colours.

As much as I love the rich, nearly black indigo of newly bought unwashed jeans, the pale grey-blue tones of soft, well-worn denim bring a comforting vibe to any room.

SOFTEN UP

Certain homes have more impact on me than others.
I can't always pinpoint why I prefer one place to
another, or why specific colours stick in my memory
more than others. I guess it all has to do with what
mood I am in at the time. Moods are unpredictable,
so it is hard to know for sure how you will feel
about certain things, but it is probably true to say
that if you were in a bad mood, your impression of
something would be very different from when you
are feeling happy. It is also the case that our moods
can be significantly lifted by certain things we find
or see, and colour definitely has that ability. Soft
colours always make me feel calm, contented, relaxed
and in a good mood. There is nothing offensive or
aggressive about them; they are simply soothing,
uplifting and inviting.

Colour has the ability to influence our mood in an instant, from bright, vibrant hues that energize and stimulate, to dark, moody shades that create a cosy, cocooning feeling. Pale, soft shades are the ultimate soothing colours that create calming, tranquil interiors.

ADD TEXTURE.

These pictures are all of the Parisian apartment featured earlier in this chapter, and they beautifully illustrate how soft colours come alive when you add contrast, texture and especially wood or woven rattan to the scheme. This combination somehow makes the soft backdrop seem even softer and enhances the colours of the natural materials. The simple setting (opposite) is a detail from the bathroom, where wooden beads adorn the towel hook and baskets holding hand-towels are displayed on a vintage wooden stool. The retro-looking chair adds a different feel alongside the wood features. The kitchen table (above left) was specially designed for the space, with custom-made metal legs that wrap around the wooden tabletop with its uneven edges. Various soft tones have been used throughout the apartment to add layers of interest. Here, the chair and sideboard (above right) have been painted in different soft colours, while the modern lamp introduces a cool vibe.

SWEET DREAMS.

Linen sheets in soft colours make a bed so inviting. Layering pale greens, muted blues and gentle greys can never go wrong as long as the shades are harmonious. I added textural interest to this setting (this page) in the form of antique glass containers with their original labels still intact, which can be used for storage or as a water bottle beside the bed. The wicker basket hangs on twine suspended between two walls, which can also double up as a place to hang clothes. Opposite is a detail of one of my favourite oil paintings by Jacqueline Dubois. We were lucky to find a few of her paintings in an antiques shop in the south of France, and I just love the colours and textures of this one.

SMOKE, MIST & RAIN

Some of nature's most beautiful moments are misty mornings and evenings, when the colours soften as a veil of mist blurs the edges of everything it covers. Summer mist tends to be light and transient, whereas on rainy days in the autumn it seems darker and heavier. Mist and rain make the colours of the surrounding landscape fade, so that everything seems to be different shades of grey. Some people find days such as this depressing, when everything has lost its definition and colour, but I find them beautiful. As a wall colour in an interior, soft grey has the opposite effect to mist, as it makes the most perfect backdrop to any other accent colour and intensifies its beauty.

MISTY FEELING.

Misty greys range from shades with a blue or black undertone to those with a hint of green. They work in harmony together, as well as with natural objects and colours, creating a pared-down but considered look. Against a grey backdrop, ash-grey duck eggs on a linen cloth resemble pebbles (opposite). A simple setting of dried branches in front of a sheer curtain can seem like a work of art (above). Hanging an oil painting with a ribbon adds an extra decorative touch (far left). An eclectic display of misty grey inspirations (left).

Because the soft, dusty paints contain a touch of black, the various tones of misty greys, both light and dark, harmonize beautifully with any other soft colour.

SOFTLY PAINTED.

If you can't find the perfect coloured terracotta pot for your plants, you can easily paint your own in any shade you like. It is easy to do, and you can mix and match lots of different colours or use only one or two, depending on the look you want. These pots are painted in a lime paint from Bauwerk Colour that is suitable for both indoors and out. The colours used here are (from left to right): Dove, Water, Sedum, Nightshade, Day, Kohlrabi, Amethyst and Duck Egg.

ELEGANTLY GREY

Smoky grey walls make any room feel supremely elegant. It is a very easy colour to work with when it comes to furnishing the space, as nearly everything looks good with grey. Whether you prefer a pared-down look or a fuller and more decorated style, you will be able to create an inviting and chic space that will be easy to live in. If you are someone who likes to change and update furniture, accessories or textiles, a grey backdrop will make things simple, as this flexible neutral works successfully with any other colour. Soft pastels will look as good against it as a scheme made up of other neutrals, and if you want to add pops of brighter colours, you won't fail either. Easy on the eye, smoky grey is a safe option for walls and I am sure you will be very happy with the result.

I highly recommend that you paint your walls smoky grey, as it is such a flexible base colour that is easy on the eye and will make your home feel very soft and up to date.

KEEP IT SIMPLE.

If the architecture of your home is attractive, one way not to detract from that is to furnish your space simply and keep it free from clutter. The bare essentials will be enough to create a space that is inviting and stylish. Consider how the Shakers furnished their homes, in a functional, pared-down style that included only the items they really needed. This lovely dining space has been decorated and furnished with a similar approach, with a simple yet beautiful antique table and chairs and a grey-painted cabinet that stores everything required for an easy breakfast or a full dinner table. Keep things simple, and let the architecture of your space be its main feature.

LEFT UNTOUCHED.

Left in its original grace and untouched for many years, this must be one of my all-time favourite houses. It belongs to the founders of the paint company Bauwerk Colour, and it is interesting to see that, even as owners of a paint company, they have not gone crazy and repainted all the walls, but instead have chosen to let them be. I love the deep-set windows, panelled shutters and painted walls that still possess their original colour and patina. The bedroom (opposite) is simply furnished with a large bed dressed in layers of soft white linen and a bronze-coloured, textured throw that adds a warm hue. The only other furniture in the room is a simple antique table and a small cabinet for storing bed linen. My dog Felix came with me to this photoshoot, and he jumped straight onto the bed and stayed there for most of the day, enjoying the space.

ORIGINAL STATE

Anyone who has read my other books will have gathered that I have a great fondness for scuffed or peeling walls. I know this is not to everyone's taste and I understand that when most people buy a house with this kind of distressed look, they want to repaint. At the same time, it makes me so happy to find an old house where no changes have been made and it has been left in its original state with layers of previous colours still intact. This pleasure is becoming increasingly rare today, as most houses have lost their timeworn patina under coats of new paint. I would love to see more houses left in this state and, if they are renovated, their original bases restored instead of being covered up.

WHEAT, CORN & FLAX

Last but not least in the soft colour range is a dusty yellow, which is a lovely choice for wall paint, painted furniture or accessories. It is easy to combine with other hues but will also work beautifully as a main feature colour. Dusty yellow is inspired by the natural tones of wheat, corn and flax, none of which are pure yellow, as they have added black and sometimes a soft green hue. I recommend choosing a shade that is not too intensely yellow. As with all soft colours, these gentle tones should have a muted feeling that ensures the result is subtle rather than bright. I invariably prefer the shades that have an almost indescribable colour, as I think that is when soft colours look their best.

TOUCHES OF SOFT YELLOW.
Soft yellow tones inspired by nature (left and far left) work well with most other colours and will brighten up dark backdrops, such as the soft greys shown here. When we moved into our flat in Paris, we found some double doors that had been hidden behind shelves and a cabinet. We left their original colour and I added extra storage in the form of a yellow-painted chair hanging on the door handle (above). I collect vintage ribbons whenever I find them, as they are useful for my work and as colour inspiration (opposite).

DIFFERENT LIGHT

A soft yellow backdrop will give your home a subtle, warm glow that will make it welcoming and inviting. Whether you prefer to decorate with warm or cool tones partly depends on the climate where you live, as this can greatly influence the colour mood you choose to work with. In a sunny part of the world, colours look very different from in a colder, darker climate. There is no right or wrong to the colours you choose, wherever you live, but it might be something worth considering. If, for example, you live in a place that is very dark, you may want to go for lighter colours; and if you live in a sunnier area, perhaps a darker colour scheme will be easier on the eye, as the surrounding light is so bright. A dusty yellow colour will work in any climate, as it will brighten up a dark environment or soften intense sunlight.

Gentle dusty yellows, such as the warm tones of wheat, corn and flax, will work well in any environment, as they help to soften bright light and are uplifting in dark spaces.

Working with different shades of colours from the same side of the colour wheel can be difficult. Traditionally, combinations such as pink and red or red and orange shouldn't really work together, but, as shown opposite, with pops of yellow thrown into the mix, they can look stylish and fun. This uplifting setting makes me think of a circus, where there is always a kaleidoscope of bright, happy colours mixed together.

Choosing a bold and bright colour scheme takes courage, as it will dominate your space and divert much of the attention from everything else in the room. At the same time, it makes a brave statement and the bright, happy colours will put a smile on your face. Bold colours usually complement each other and so mix well, and can be used to accessorize a light or dark home. If you use a bright colour scheme for the backdrop, dark furniture and furnishings can be added to create a look that is not bold through and through. I love visiting a home with a bold colour scheme, as it is such a personal choice, and one thing is for sure: it will stand out among all the neutral interiors.

BOLD

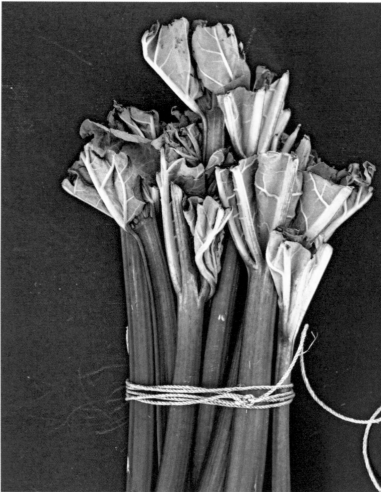

BOLD INSPIRATIONS

When it comes to nature, bold colours mostly appear in moderation. Of course, there are some exceptions, but you are more likely to find small bursts of happy colours rather than large expanses of bright hues. My view is that if you mimic the way bold colours are used in nature when you are decorating your home, the result will be very successful. I always find it so exciting when the dark winter days become brighter and lighter, and nature explodes into colours that announce to the world that spring is here. From the moment the trees produce their first light green leaves to when fields of poppies and rapeseed flowers brighten up the landscape, it makes all the difference to my mood and gives me a renewed boost of energy. Using bold colours in the home can have a similar energizing effect, as it will always feel like spring has just arrived.

Much like the joyful chaos and flamboyance of a circus, nature's kaleidoscope of bright,
happy colours cannot fail to put a smile on your face. Full of optimism and energy,
a bold, bright palette will make your home feel like it is spring all year round.

NATURALLY BOLD.

There are many bold colour inspirations to be found in the natural world in every
season, but it is during the spring and summer months when gardens, fields and country
roadsides really explode into colour. Foliage is lush and abundant, flowers come into
bloom and it is a joy to be able to pick them from the garden to brighten up our homes.
The range of bold colours found in nature covers the whole of the colour wheel and you
can find almost any shade, from sky-blue flowers and deep pink rhubarb to bright red
berries and golden orange fruits. All of these vivid colours make us happy when they
appear, even though they are only with us for a short length of time.

The range of bold hues found in nature covers the whole colour wheel and you can find almost any shade imaginable to get inspired by, from sky-blue cornflowers, rich red poppies and bright yellow rapeseed flowers, to raspberries, oranges and limes.

COLOUR COLLECTION.

If I could make them last, I would collect flowers as colour inspiration, as there is no better source of naturally produced bold hues. Luckily, there are many other things to use as colour inspiration, such as these silk threads in the most extraordinary vibrant colours. I buy them whenever I see them at a flea market, as they make beautiful decorations and give any interior a fabulous bold colour injection. If you have as many as I do, you can store them in a glass vase and they will have a similar effect to a large bunch of flowers.

HYACINTH & SUMMER SKIES

It is sometimes hard to know why we like certain things more than others, why some things make us feel happy or sad, or why we prefer one colour to another. Blue is my colour, but if you were to ask me why, the only explanation I would be able to give is that my two favourite flowers are grape hyacinths (*Muscari*, above right) and forget-me-nots, and I love their rich saturated blue tones. They were my grandmother's flowers of choice too; her garden was full of them in spring and I remember exactly how beautiful it looked. I loved spending time with her and these flowers remind me so much of her that they bring back wonderful memories.

SUMMER COLOUR.

Although my favourite flowers, grape hyacinths (above), appear in spring, together with wonderfully scented hyacinths (left), I always associate the colour blue with summer – for the hot, sunny days with blue sky overhead. Painting your walls a deep blue will give you a sense of summer all year round, and you can add warmth with natural objects and colours (opposite). The console table and botanical prints were designed and produced by Drythings, and the furniture and accessories are flea-market finds.

If I were to label the seasons by colour, I would say that summer is blue — for the deep blue skies that I love — autumn is muddy tones, winter is white and spring is green.

DIFFERENT SHADES.

I could happily live in a completely blue room, as it would have such a soothing and calming atmosphere. Blue is a colour that works especially well when you layer up different shades to create a tone-on-tone effect, resulting in a harmonious interior with a sense of depth. The shiny silk-covered sofa (opposite) brings texture and a touch of glamour to this otherwise pared-down space, where the only thing that is needed to bring it all together is a large vase of glossy leaves. Using a slightly darker blue backdrop with lighter furniture and accessories is a great way to make an interesting feature in your home (above left). Another equally effective option is to use the same shade on both the walls and the furniture to create a monochrome effect (above right). Leaving one feature wall with peeling wallpaper among plain-coloured surrounding walls will add texture and interest to your home (right).

BOTTLE GREEN & VERDIGRIS

I don't know how it came about that green is the colour we use to describe envy. The saying could just as easily have been, 'I am yellow with envy'. But none of this matters when it comes to working with shades of green in the home because it is such a wonderful colour to live with, similar to being in a tranquil, leaf-covered forest. Just imagine how amazing it would be to live high up in a treehouse, surrounded by trees and their canopy of leaves. Bold green hues range from the lighter greens of new shoots to the darker greens of lush moss; some shades flirt a little with blue, while others have a purer green tone, but they all create a very calming atmosphere when used in the home.

SHADES OF GREEN.

So many shades of bold green look amazing in interiors. I recommend using darker tones as the backdrop and the brighter shades as accents, as they can be quite invasive if used on a large scale. Green colours are easy to mix – just look to nature for inspiration. A shaded green-painted or papered wall will work beautifully as a backdrop for darker green tones and pale colours alike, such as this simple trestle desk in front of wallpaper by Designers Guild (opposite).

GOING GREEN.

This otherwise white kitchen has been updated with a collection of furniture and accessories in different tints of green. The antique table and chairs define the central space, while vintage china and stone pots make a decorative feature displayed on shelves or hung on the walls. The old kitchen previously had only open storage, but it has been updated with a heavy linen cloth, dyed a bluish-green shade, instead of cabinet doors. This keeps the shelves free from dust and also adds a soft, tactile element to the space, which could otherwise feel quite sterile and hard. The layers of different shades of green harmonize beautifully and give the space a multi-tonal effect, all from within the same colour family.

MIMOSA, SUNFLOWER & MARIGOLD

One of spring's most beautiful sights is a field of dazzling yellow rapeseed flowers, only matched in summer by an array of sunflowers with their heads all turned towards the sun. The most uplifting of hues, yellow instantly makes me happy and brings brightness and a feeling of summer. I recommend using it on walls, floors and even ceilings. It complements most colours, so you have the choice of adding other bright hues or toning it down with neutrals and pale accents. It is a colour you don't often see in interiors, but I hope the following pages will make you consider it. This summery shade will create such a happy mood that I am sure you won't regret choosing it for your home.

HELLO SUNSHINE.

Can you imagine living in an interior with a year-round summery feeling? Being greeted by a sunshine-yellow wall would always make you smile. The home office (opposite) has been co-ordinated by using the same hue on both the wall and desk, along with natural wood furniture and woven materials for a layered, up-to-date look. The leather-backed bentwood chair came from the Gemla factory near my home town, and the poppy poster is from Drythings. Flowers and vegetables are a great source of yellow colour inspiration (this page).

A VARIETY OF YELLOWS

When it comes to choosing a bold yellow colour for your home, you can either go for a clear, bright shade inspired by sunflowers and rapeseed flowers, or opt for a dirtier mustard tone. All yellows work equally well as the main and accent colours, but pure yellow shades will result in a lighter and brighter interior, whereas duller, greener yellows will create a slightly moodier look, so your choice is all down to the effect you are hoping to achieve. To my mind, you can never really go wrong when you choose a yellow colour scheme for your home, as it will always give you a happy outlook and be comfortable to live with.

ADDING TEXTILES.

Introducing coloured textiles is an easy way to brighten up an interior. A length of canvas painted in a favourite shade and nailed to the wall will create a backdrop for any still life, while also adding contrasting colour (this page). Bright yellow bed linen will guarantee you wake up in a sunny mood every day (opposite). The vintage metal chair makes an unusual bedside table and the old shutter, painted in raspberry, adds another bold colour and a layer of warmth to this industrial space.

YOUR CHOICE.

Bright yellow shades are easy to mix in with most colours, whether you choose similar bold hues, such as raspberry, orange or blue, or shades from the softer colour range, as shown here, where the grey bed linen on the white four-poster bed calms down the bright yellow wall. It may seem hard to know how to work with colours in your home and how to pair them together successfully, but there really are no rules about what is right or wrong. I think you just have to try and see what you feel comfortable with. The colour scheme you opt for might not be what someone else would choose, but that isn't important. You are the designer of your own look, and only you can decide when you have created the home you want to live in. My best advice is to go with your gut feeling – it is normally the right way to go.

YELLOW IS BEAUTIFUL.

In Sweden, we have rhyming sayings about colour. One is *gult är fult*, which translates to 'yellow is ugly'; another is *blått är flott*, which means 'blue is elegant'. I certainly don't agree that yellow is ugly – in fact, I'd say the opposite is true: yellow is a beautiful colour. I don't think the sayings hold any truth, they are just a play on rhyming words, yet it is interesting that these sayings are used, because who could ever say that daffodils aren't a beautiful colour, whether fresh or dried (opposite)? The same is true of this textural kitchen wall, which has been painted in such a wonderful shade of summery yellow. Against this stunning backdrop, the herbs and vegetables and other kitchen paraphernalia on the side table look like a still life.

RASPBERRY, ORANGE & PEONY

I realized how beautiful strong colours can be during my first trip to Mexico, where I saw them used with great success on both the exterior and interior of houses. In my opinion, bright colours look best when they have weathered a little and become slightly muted. This effect is, of course, hard to achieve when repainting your walls, but one tip is to use a very matt finish, which gives a bold colour more depth and ensures it isn't uncomfortably vibrant. I noticed that a lot of houses in Mexico were painted in warm tones, such as orange, red and raspberry, and it made me realize how much I love these colours, both on larger surfaces and in smaller doses in textiles and accessories.

GOING BOLD.

Bold colours can seem daunting, especially for anyone used to living with neutrals. Experiment by adding rugs, cushions or bed linen, or paint a feature wall in your chosen hue to see how it feels to live with. I test colours by painting a large canvas and taping it to the wall; then I add some accessories to see how I like the look (opposite). Using a textile or rug as wall art is an easy way to bring colour into your home (above). Vintage arrows, found in an antique shop in Arizona, make a unique still life on a side table (left).

Ease yourself in to the idea of using bold tones by adding colourful textiles, rugs, cushions or bed linen, and experiment by painting one feature wall before going all the way.

BOLD FEATURES.

There are many ways to add bold colours to your home, and if you don't feel ready to paint your walls or floors, you can start with some smaller areas. Painting a door is one way to create a colourful focal point in your home; it will also help you to decide how much more colour to add or whether you want to keep it to the bare minimum. These double doors (opposite) have been painted in a deep orange colour, and the different shades of orange together with the raspberries on the small table in front illustrate how well these similar warm tones work together. Another successful combination is orange and denim blue, as seen in this collection of colourful threads (right). A fabric or rug displayed on a wall is a great way to introduce colour and easy to update when you want a new look. The striped soft-woven Bolivian *frazada* is from my new favourite shop BON in Tucson, Arizona, and the grey antique cabinet is from Sweden (above right).

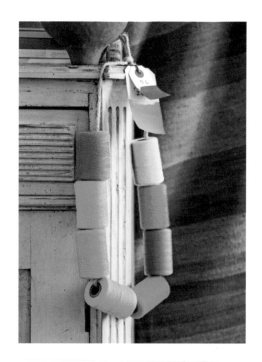

SOFTLY PINK.

I would not hesitate to paint a room or a feature wall in one of the dirtier shades of raspberry, as it is a colour that can be very elegant and also quite easy to mix with other hues. Here, the soft pink shades of the hydrangeas, the watery deep blue of the glass vase and the pale grey of the tabletop are all offset beautifully by the wall painted in Radicchio by Farrow & Ball (left).

SCRUFFY FEATURE.

Leaving a section of a wall in a scruffy state, with layers of flaking paint from previous decorating jobs, will add extra interest and make a colourful feature that is both unique and personal. In this living space (right), I especially like how the distressed coloured paintwork frames the large industrial window and ties in with the raspberry-coloured sofa and still life on the folding metal table.

GOING FOR RASPBERRY

The world is so full of colour and it is strange to think that although we see them all, we don't always have a relationship with certain shades. Perhaps we are so used to them that we don't even consider how they could be used in our homes. Raspberry is one such colour. I have never used it for a job or in my own home, but while working on this book I realized it is a colour I like and I wonder why I have never used it before. It is a bold shade, but also very soft, which makes it soothing rather than overwhelming. As with many hues, there are certain raspberry shades that are bolder and brighter than others, so I would always opt for one with a touch of black in it, as the moody tone will give a more elegant result.

The Poppy Series

{ *lat. Papaver* }

Pose №9

DRY THINGS IN COLLABORATION WITH
Ewa-Marie Rundquist

ADDING COLOUR.

The raspberry-pink paint used on the wall opposite is a bright hue, but its effect has been slightly toned down by the large poster depicting papery poppies on a greyish background. The tray and poster are both from Drythings. Textiles and upholstered furniture are great ways to bring strong, bold colours into an interior (this page). I love the oversized flower arrangement against the shiny curtain, as it adds a bit of over-the-top decadence to the colourful corner featured here.

ADDRESS BOOK

UK

THE CLOTH SHOP
290 Portobello Road
London W10 5TE
+44 (0)208 968 6001
www.theclothshop.net
With a large selection of fabrics, linen and quilts, this shop is a must if you are a textile lover.

FARROW & BALL
www.farrow-ball.com
One of my favourite paint manufacturers.

LABOUR AND WAIT
85 Redchurch Street
London E2 7DJ
+44 (0)20 7729 6253
www.labourandwait.co.uk
A large selection of beautifully curated household ware and accessories.

LITTLE GREENE
www.littlegreene.com
A large range of paint colours with subtlety and depth of colour.

QUIRKY INTERIORS
1 Stonecross
St Albans
Herts AL1 4AA
+44 (0)7890 262247
www.quirkyinteriors.co.uk
A company that specializes in industrial and vintage furniture, aged zinc and other vintage items. Check out their handmade copper tiles on page 31.

USA

ABC CARPET & HOME
888 Broadway
New York, NY 10003
+1 212 473 3000
www.abchome.com
A must-visit when you are in New York. It is one of the most inspiring shops – I can spend hours in here.

BENJAMIN MOORE
www.benjaminmoore.com
A paint company with a large range of beautiful colours.

BON BOUTIQUE
760 S Stone Avenue
Tucson, AZ 85701
+1 520 795 2272
www.bon-boutique.com
A new favourite of mine, selling ceramics, baskets, frazada blankets, fabrics and gift items.

JOHN DERIAN
6 East Second Street
New York, NY 10003
+1 212 677 3917
www.johnderian.com
One of my all-time favourite stores, where you can find découpaged plates, furniture, decorative accessories and fabrics both old and new.

FRONT GENERAL STORE
143 Front Street
Brooklyn, NY 11201
+1 347 693 5328
www.frontgeneralstore.com
Vintage homewares, accessories and clothing. A great shop for discovering things you won't find anywhere else.

GREEN FINGERS MARKET
5 Rivington Street
New York, NY 10002
www.greenfingersnyc.com
Plants, vintage accessories, vintage clothing and Japanese indigo fabrics and scarves.

HOLLER & SQUALL
119 Atlantic Avenue
Brooklyn, NY 11201
www.hollerandsquall.com
A great collection of vintage and antique American furniture, accessories and lamps – a must if you are searching for something special or unusual.

THE HUDSON MERCANTILE
318 Warren Street
Hudson, NY 12534
One of the best antique shops in Hudson, with a selection of American furniture and accessories.

THE MART COLLECTION
1600 Lincoln Blvd
Venice, CA 90291
www.themartcollective.com
An antique mart that's home to 85 dealers and is a great source for everything vintage, from furniture to decorative accessories and textiles.

RED CHAIR ON WARREN
606 Warren Street
Hudson, NY 12534
+1 518 828 1158
www.redchair-antiques.com
This gorgeous store specializes in French antiques with a large selection of furniture, homeware, French linen cloths and fabrics imported from France.

FRANCE

L'OBJET QUI PARLE
86 Rue des Martyrs
75018 Paris
www.objetquiparle.com
Quirky vintage things to add to your collections, with everything from kitchenware to vintage wallpapers to stuffed birds and antique glass cloches.

MERCI
111 Boulevard Beaumarchais
75003 Paris
www.merci-merci.com
Stylish lifestyle store selling clothing, accessories and homewares, including a large collection of table and bed linen of the finest quality in a beautiful range of colours.

CARAVANE
www.caravane.fr
Furniture, fabrics, lighting, rugs and a paint collection with a large range of colours.

SWEDEN

ARTILLERIET INTERIORS AB
Magasinsgatan 19
411 18 Göteborg
www.artelleriet.se
An eclectic selection of homewares, furniture and accessories and a place you must visit if you are in Gothenburg.

DRYTHINGS
Upplandsgatan 36
11328 Stockholm
www.drythings.se
A well-designed range of furniture, graphic and photographic posters, chopping boards and bags (see page 179).

EVENSEN ANTIK
Upplandsgatan 40
11328 Stockholm
www.brukthandel.se
Swedish antique furniture and vintage accessories. I always find great props here.

GARBO INTERIORS
Brahegatan 21
114 37 Stockholm
www.garbointeriors.com
Antique and modern furniture, textiles and paints.

GEMLA FURNITURE
www.gemlaab.se
A 150-year-old furniture company located close to my childhood home that produces beautiful, timeless furniture and bentwood chairs that I just love (see page 187). Visit their website for details of stockists.

KARDELEN LINEN
www.kardelen.se
Linen for every room in your house (see pages 54 and 68).

L&K ANTIQUES
www.gustafssonhb.com
Scandinavian antique furniture from the 18th and 19th centuries (see pages 72–73).

SANDBERGS WALLPAPER
www.sandbergswallpaper.com
A large range of wallpapers, from florals to simple stripes.

THE NETHERLANDS & BELGIUM
ELLIE CASHMAN DESIGN
www.elliecashmandesign.com
Beautiful oversized floral wallpapers, fabrics and cushions. Will make a grand statement in any home (see pages 144–145).

COULEUR LOCALE
www.couleurlocale.eu
Baskets, wooden items, tableware, lighting and textiles, sourced mostly in Africa.

FLAMANT
www.flamant.com
Beautiful paint colours.

SOUTH AFRICA
KOÖPERASIE STORIES
R45 Road between Paarl and Franschhoek
Simondium 7670
www.kooperasiestories.co.za
A large selection of vintage and antique furniture, accessories and linen cloths and sacks. A must-visit if you're in Cape Town.

STUDIO IRA BEKKER
www.studioirabekker.co.za
Eco-friendly printed linen and cotton textiles with the most beautiful patterns and colours. The collection includes table linen, cushions and bags (see pages 28–29).

WOODSTOCK VINTAGE
131 Sir Lowry Road
Woodstock
Cape Town 7925
This vintage furniture shop is probably my favourite store in Cape Town. I always find something different and interesting here.

AUSTRALIA
BAUWERK COLOUR
www.bauwerkcolour.com
Lime paint for indoor and outdoor use in the most beautiful colours and texture. Stockists of my new paint range of nine specially designed colours!

BUSINESS CREDITS

PAOLO BADESCO INTERIOR DESIGN
Viale di Porta Vercellina, 5
20123 Milan
Italy
www.paolobadesco.it
www.rawmilano.it
and
Lamps by DCW (France)
Wall paints by The Paint Makers Company (Italy)
Pages 54, 130 left, 131 left.

BAUWERK COLOUR
PO Box 599
South Freemantle
WA 6162
Australia
T: +61 8 9433 3860
and
15 Haupstrasse
Oelzschau bei
Belgem 04874
Germany
T: +49 152 5537 1203
E: info@bauwerkcolour.com
www.bauwerkcolour.com.au
Pages 2, 4, 39, 98, 105, 107, 111–113, 116–117, 120–121, 158 above, 160–161, 164–165, 166–167.

MARIANNE COTTERILL
Location available for hire
www.mariannecotterill.com
www.mapesburyroad.com
Pages 45 above left, 135, 146, 180, 188, 201.

FIL DE FER
Store Kongensgade 83 A
1264 Copenhagen
Denmark
T: +45 33 32 32 46
E: shop@fildefercph.com
www.fildefercph.com
Pages 48–49.

**LARS GUSTAFSSON
L&K ANTIQUES**
Gemlagatan 1
34371 Diö
Sweden
www.gustafssonhb.com
Instagram: @landkantiques
Pages 72–73, 148 left.

BÉNÉDICTE LEUWERS
Antique dealer, interior designer, set designer, home styling, event styling and design.
Showroom:
15 Quai Jean Javres
84800 L'Isle sur la Sorgue
France
T: +33 7 81 16 38 28
By appointment only from Monday–Sunday
Instagram:_benedicte_ benedicte
www.benedicte.eu
Pages 70, 80, 83 right, 86–87, 122–123, 152–153, 182 above, 182 below left, 184–185.

FILIPPA ROSENQVIST
RÖSTER Voices Places Faces
Full service production company for national and international clients in Stockholm, Sweden.
E: filippa@roster.se
www.roster.se
Pages 178 below left, 179, 186–187, 200.

CHEZ MARIE SIXTINE
www.marie-sixtine.com
A cosy secret hideaway nestled above the shop of the same name used by journalists, VIPs, etc. for meetings and events.

**INTERIOR DESIGN BY
SANDRINE PLACE AND
ATELIER BAPTISTE LEGUÉ**
www.sandrineplace.com
www.baptistelegue.com
Wall painted by Alexandre
Poulaillon
www.atelier-poulaillon.com/
papiers-dominotes/papiers-
dominotes/

www.whole.fr
www.eu.farrow-ball.com
*Pages 36, 128, 138–139,
154–155.*

DEBI TRELOAR
www.debitreloar.com
*Pages 1, 29, 88, 92–93, 136,
158 below left, 163, 170–171,
181, 190–191, 205.*

WALL&DECÒ
Via Santerno 9,
Savio di Cervia
(RA) – Italy
Showroom: Via Solera
Mantegazza 7
Milan
Italy
T: +39 (0)544 918012
E: info@wallanddeco.com
www.wallanddeco.com
Front cover, page 53.

YEABRIDGE HOUSE
Available for location hire
from Mark Homewood
E: markhomewood@me.com
www.yeabridgehouse.com
or www.lightlocations.co.uk
*Pages 14, 22, 57, 75, 140–141,
151, 162.*

PICTURE CREDITS

INDEX

Page numbers in italic refer to the illustrations and their captions

A

accent colours *118–21*, 119, 124, *124–7*, 130
artworks, wall art 76, *76–7*

B

backdrops
    blue *180–1*, 181
    contrasting colours 49
    dark colours *38*, *40–7*, 42
    yellow 171, *171–2*
Barcelona 12
Bauwerk Colour 8, *8–9*, *38*, 99, 112, 117, 121, 161, 167
bed linen
    dark colours *27*, *49*, *55*
    pale colours *59*, *68*, 69
    soft colours *157*, 157
Bekker, Ira 29
Benjamin Moore *8*
black 37
blue *9*
    backdrops *180–1*, 181
    dark colours 18, *18–23*
    hyacinth and summer skies 178, *178–81*
    layering colours *24–7*, 25, *180–1*, 181
    natural colours 99
    pistachio, duck egg and faded denim *146–53*, 147
bold colours 172–201
    bottle green and verdigris 182, *182–5*
    doors *196*, 197
    green *118–21*, 119
    hyacinth and summer skies 178, *178–81*
    inspiration 174–5, *174–5*
    layering *180–1*, 181
    mimosa, sunflower and marigold 186, *186–93*, 188, 190

raspberry, orange and peony 194, *194–201*
BON, Tucson, Arizona 197
bright colours *see* bold colours
brown
    hazelnut, terracotta and wood 104, *104–7*
    natural colours 30, 99

C

cactus green 110, *110–11*
Cape Town 12, 29
Cashman, Ellie 144
china *64–5*, *89*, 90, *90*, *94–5*
clay 30, *30–5*
clothes rails 67
contrasting colours 48–51, 49, *82–7*, 83
copper tiles *31*

D

dark colours 14–57
    backdrops *38*, *40–7*, 42
    blue 18, *18–23*
    clay, earth and mud 30, *30–5*
    contrasting colours *48–51*, 49
    forest, moss and pine 52, *52–5*
    inspirations 16–17, *16–17*
    layering *24–7*, 25
    light and *14*, 15
    linen fabrics *28–9*, 29
    thunder, charcoal and night *36–41*, 37
denim blue 18, 25, 142, 147, *152–3*
Designers Guild *182*
displays
    dark colours *34*
    mirrors *70*, 71
    pale colours *62*, *64–5*
distressed walls *166–7*, 167, *198–9*
doors, bold colours *196*, 197
Drythings *178*, *201*

Dubois, Jacques *156*, 157
duck-egg blue 147, 148, *148–9*
dusky shades
    soft colours 140, *140–3*
    yellow 168, *168–9*
Dutch paintings 45
dyes, linen fabrics *28–9*, 29

E

Earthborn *34*
earthy colours 30, *30–5*

F

fabrics
    adding softness 66
    denim 18, 152
    floral fabrics *136–7*, 137
    loose covers *85*, *85*
    pale colours *59*, 80, *80–1*
    table linen 90, *90*
    texture 49
    wall hangings 197, *197*
    yellow 188, *188–9*
    see also linen fabrics
Farrow & Ball 8, *18*, *34*, 45, 51, *62*, 198
Flamant *18*, *34*
flowers 124
    blue 178, *178*
    bold colours 175, 177, *201*
    floral fabrics *136–7*, 137
    soft colours 130, *132–4*
    yellow 186, *186*, *191–2*
focal points, dark backdrops 42, 45
forest colours 52, *52–5*
France 12, 74, 76, 80
furniture
    loose covers *85*, *85*
    natural colours 104
    pale colours *69*
    Swedish 72, *72–5*

G

geraniums, scented *56–7*, 57
green

bottle green and verdigris 182, *182–5*
forest, moss and pine 52, *52–5*
natural colours 99
olive, cactus and sage 110, *110–11*
pistachio 147, 149
plants *56–7*, 57, 84, *84*, 124, *124–6*
spring, fig and apple *118–21*, 119
tonal layering *122–3*, 123
grey
    linen fabrics 51
    natural colours 99
    smoke, mist and rain 158, *158–63*
    thunder, charcoal and night *36–41*, 37

H

hyacinth blue *178*

I

indigo 18, 25, 152
inspiration
    bold colours 174–5, *174–5*
    dark colours 16–17, *16–17*
    natural colours 100, *100–1*
    pale colours 60–1, *60–1*
    soft colours 130–1, *130–1*
    sources of *11–13*

K

Kardelen *55*, *162*

L

layering colours
    blue *180–1*, 181
    dark colours *24–7*, 25
    natural colours 112, *112–13*
    pale colours 66, *66–9*, 69
    soft colours 138, *138–9*, 157, *157*
    tonal layering *122–3*, 123

light
    and dark colours *14*, 15, 42,
        42–3, 45
    mirrors 71
    yellow backdrops 171
linen fabrics
    dark colours *28–9*, 29
    grey-dyed 51
    pale colours *59*, 62, 67, 80,
        80–1
Little Greene 8, *18*, 25, 62,
    102, *132*, *136*, *162*, *171*
loose covers 85, *85*

M
Merci, Paris 149
Mexico *11–13*, 194
mirrors *70*, 71, 86, *87*
mist 158
mixing colours 121
monochrome schemes
    blue *22–3*
    texture 86, *86–7*
    white 59
moody colours *see* dark colours
mossy colours 52, *54–5*, 55
muddy colours 30, *30–5*

N
natural colours *98–127*
    accent colours *118–21*, 119,
        124, *124–7*
    bold colours 174, *174–5*
    colour combinations 114,
        114–15
    dark colours 16–17,
        16–17
    hazelnut, terracotta and
        wood 104, *104–7*
    inspirations 100, *100–1*
    layering 112, *112–13*
    olive, cactus and sage 110,
        110–11
    pale colours 60–1, *60–1*
    plants *56–7*, *57*
    soft colours 130–1, *130–1*

spring, fig and apple
    118–21, 119
    texture *104–9*, 108
    tonal layering *122–3*, 123

O
oiling wood 108
olive green 110, *110–11*
orange 194, *196–7*, 197

P
pale colours *58–97*
    adding softness 66, *66–7*
    china 90, *90*, *94–5*
    contrasting colours *82–7*, 83
    fabrics *59*
    ice, cloud and snow *88–9*, 89
    inspirations 60–1, *60–1*
    ivory, string and parchment
        62, *62–5*
    Swedish furniture 72, *72–5*
    table linen 90, *90*
    texture *59*, 62, 69, 83, 86,
        86–7
    washed, bleached and
        weathered 78, *78–81*, 80
Paris 149, 155
pastel colours *see* soft colours
Perers, Kristin *25*
pine trees 52
pink
    dusky shades 140, *140–3*
    raspberry 194, 198, *198–201*
    rose, powder and petal 132,
        132–3
pistachio green *147*, 149
plants *56–7*, 57, 84, *84*, 124,
    124–6
pots, terracotta *160–1*
Poulaillon, Alexandre *138–9*

R
rain 158
raspberry 194, 198, *198–201*
RAW Milano 52
recipe wall 91, *91*

red 194, *194–7*
Riedel, Bronwyn and Andreas
    8
roses *132*, *142–3*, 143

S
sage green 110, *110–11*
Sanderson *132*
Shakers 165
simplicity 165
Sixtine, Marie *128*, *138–9*
smoky grey 162, *162–3*
snow 60, 89
soft colours *128–71*
    bed linen 157, *157*
    decorated walls 144, *144–5*
    distressed walls *166–7*, 167
    dusky shades 140, *140–3*
    floral fabrics *136–7*, 137
    inspirations 130–1, *130–1*
    layering 138, *138–9*, 157,
        157
    pistachio, duck egg and
        faded denim *146–53*, 147
    rose, powder and petal 132,
        132–3
    smoke, mist and rain 158,
        158–63
    wheat, corn and flax 168,
        168–9
    yellow backdrops 171, *171–2*
spring colours 119
Stockholm 12
Sweden 59, *72–5*, 89, 193, 197

T
table settings
    natural colours *102–3*
    white 90, *90*
terracotta pots *160–1*
textiles *see* fabrics
texture *13*
    fabrics 49
    natural colours *104–9*, 108
    pale colours *59*, 62, 69, 83,
        86, *86–7*

plants 57
thunder grey 37
tiles, copper *31*
tonal layering *122–3*, 123
tonal walls *38*
Treloar, Debi *89*, *92*
Tulum *12*

W
Wall & Decò *52*
walls
    distressed walls *166–7*, 167,
        198–9
    recipe wall 91, *91*
    smoky grey 162, *162–3*
    soft colours 144, *144–5*
    two-tone 112, *112–13*
    wall art 76, *76–7*
    wallpaper 144, *144*
weather *36*, 37, 60
white 59, 62
    china 89, 90, *90*, *94–5*
    ice, cloud and snow *88–9*, 89
    table linen 90, *90*
    texture 86, *86–7*
    see also pale colours
windows, and dark colours
    14, 15
winter colours 60, 89
wood 104, *104*
    oiling 108
    texture *106–9*, 108
    weathered 78, *79*

Y
yellow
    backdrops 171, *171–2*
    mimosa, sunflower and
        marigold 186, *186–93*,
        188, 190
    wheat, corn and flax 168,
        168–9

DEBI TRELOAR You are simply the best. I love working with you and I am so grateful to have you as a very dear and close friend.

FREDERICK AND FELIX Thank you for being so patient with me turning our home upside down and spending hours with my camera and for always being there helping me out. Love you both.

WOODY HOLDING For being so kind and for always helping out your mum and me when we are working together.

ANNABEL MORGAN Without you my books wouldn't be what they are, you are the best editor I could ever wish for.

MEGAN, LESLIE, JESS, ZIA AND CINDY Thank you for making this possible, for always being open to ideas and for working so hard to make my books beautiful and fun to work on.

FILIPPA ROSENQVIST Thank you for always finding solutions that make things possible and for being the best producer and a dear friend.

ALL THE HOME OWNERS Thank you for opening your homes and being so kind as to let me feature your worlds in my world. I am so grateful to you for your kindness and generosity.

ALL THE COMPANIES Thank you for so kindly lending me products to feature in this book – I am very grateful as they have made the book even better.

MUM AND DAD Thank you for always being here for me and for being so kind and helping us out in every possible way. Love you.